THE BIG BOOK OF RELATIONSHIP QUIZZES

THE BIG BOOK OF RELATIONSHIP QUIZZES

100 Tests and Quizzes to Let You Know Who's Who in Your Life

By Robin Westen

BLACK DOG
& LEVENTHAL
PUBLISHERS
NEW YORK

Published by
Black Dog & Leventhal Publishers, Inc.
151 West 19th Street
New York, NY 10011
www.blackdogandleventhal.com

Distributed by
Workman Publishing Company
225 Varick Street
New York, NY 10014

Manufactured in China

Cover and interior design by 3&Co.
Cover illustration by Patricia Ridgway
Interior illustrations by 3&Co., Patricia Ridgway, Dodeskaden, Heather McGrath, Jennifer Borton, Brian Landis, Fanelie Rosier, Li Kim Goh, Er Ten Hong, Kim Freitas, Anasvari, Vanda Grigorovic, Magdalena Tworkowska, Dimensions Designs, Chih-Hang Chung, Johanna Zunino, Hywit Dimyadi, Kathy Konkle, MG&Co.

ISBN-13: 978-1-57912-792-3

h g f e d c b a

Library of Congress Cataloging-in-Publication Data is on file at Black Dog & Leventhal Publishers, Inc.

Dedication

To the women who have seen me through: my mom, Millie;

my sister, Sandy; and my closest friends and confidantes—

Beth, Elsa, Helene, Janie, Laurel, Marti, Noree, and Suz

CONTENTS

PART 3
GENERAL INSIGHTS

INTRODUCTION

It's no coincidence you're reading *The Big Book of Relationship Quizzes*. For most women, relationships are the epicenter of our life. How we relate to our lovers, friends, family members, neighbors, colleagues—even pets and strangers—defines our world. Our relationships not only remind us about who we are and help to set our priorities, but as countless studies and surveys have confirmed, they also determine our deep-down happiness. When all is going well, we sail along in the breeze. But if there's any turbulence, we feel adrift. Of course, it makes sense to believe we're the captain of our own ship and in charge of steering ourselves along the sea of love. But like the nature of relationships, it's not that simple. The truth is, we're not exactly in control; we don't have *that* much choice. Biology plays a huge role in our heartfelt preoccupation.

Here's how it works: While still in utero, boys get a testosterone surge that shrinks their brain centers responsible for communication, observation, and processing emotion. (If you've ever wondered why he just doesn't *get it*—now you know.) Yet, there's no shutdown for us. In fact, we light up. During the first three months of life, for example, our ability to make eye contact and understand facial expressions increases by over 400 percent. Girls take meaning from the reactions of others—whether it's a look, or a touch, or the sound of a voice. Boys? Well, forget it. They're novices.

So here we are from the get-go, playing with dolls and creating make-believe families. We let ourselves fall head over heels with the idea of romantic love. Men may be focused on the thrill of the search, sexual conquests, driving at breakneck speed, or hitting a grand slam, but most women are looking for *true love*. And again, this goal isn't so easy. Women may desire a strong relationship, but we have a harder time forgetting hurts and slights.

A new study out of the State University of New York at Stony Brook, suggests that women's brains are wired to both feel and recall emotions more keenly than are the brains of men. It may be why we never forget our anniversaries ... but your husband? Well, give him a break. Every now and then we need to remind ourselves, despite the message of romantic movies and novels, we're all living in the real world and, sad to say, no one is perfect.

The renowned German poet Rainer Maria Rilke had it right when he wrote: "For one human being to love another; that is perhaps the most difficult of all our tasks, the ultimate, the last test and proof, the work for which all other work is but preparation." This book is a great place to start doing just that work. And here's even better news: It's easy—and *fun*!

The Big Book of Relationship Quizzes is divided into three sections. The first, and the one many women will claim is the most compelling, is "Boyfriends, Husbands, Lovers, Others." Here, the quizzes range from "What Kind of Man Do You Attract?" and "Test Your Knowledge of the Opposite Sex" to "Is It *Really* Love?" "The Marriage Clues in Your Valentine's Gift," "Which Hollywood Hottie Would Be a Perfect Match?" "Rate Your Sex Appeal," "Could an Affair Threaten Your Relationship?" and "Would You Marry for Money?" Plus, there are dozens more quizzes that explore every aspect of romantic relationships. If you have questions about whether your love will last, if you're a fool for love, or if you want to know how easy you are to live with, you'll find a quiz that offers solid insight with helpful tips on how to move your relationship in a positive direction.

The second section explores your relationships with "Friends, Family, Colleagues, and Confidants." The importance of these close ties cannot be underestimated. According to several studies, a strong network of close friends and family boosts the immune system and ultimately increases longevity. Researchers suspect that these relationships can influence our health choices, discouraging smoking or drinking as well as encouraging exercise and better dietary choices. Plus, connection with friends, family, and coworkers can also boost your mood, self-esteem, and ability to deal with life's inevitable losses.

Close friends not only provide comfort and companionship, they also help us reflect on what's truly important in our lives, offer motivation to stay focused, keep us in line so we avoid making mistakes, and forgive us when we don't take their smart advice. And let's not forget: good buddies make us laugh! If we're lucky, they're not only honest but tactful and compassionate.

But where do *you* stand as a friend? These tests will tell you. Discover "What Kind of Friend Are You?" "The True Reason Friends, Family, Neighbors, and Coworkers Love You!" and "How Do You Get Your Message Across?" as well as "What Kind of First Impression Do You Make?" and "Do You Have a Way With Animals?" But why stop there? "Are You Good Mommy Material?" "Have You Been Typecast?" and "What Kind of Advice Do You Give?"

Many of these quizzes take a unique yet research-based approach. For instance, you can find out the kind of friend you are by choosing your favorite movie snack, or by identifying with the television "friend" you miss most. Did you know there are clues to the way you relate to others in a box of chocolates? Or friendship secrets hidden in your favorite pizza? But before you bite off more than you can chew, take a break and delve into the "General Insights" section.

In this third section, you can take quizzes devoted to looking deeper into your psyche. They range from "Do You Try Too Hard to Please?" "Just How Patient With Others Are You?" "Do You Have the 'Compassion Gene'?" and "What's Your Unique Allure?" to "The Personality Clues in Your Salad," "The Secrets Hidden under Your Covers!" and "Which Colors Accentuate Your Social Self?"

If you've ever wondered whether you're too demanding, you court danger, you're mysterious, or you're an approval junkie—the answers are here. And, as in the other sections, there's plenty of research and expert advice to back up the test findings.

It's also enjoyable and engaging to give these tests to your friends and loved ones. In other words, there's lots for everyone to learn. Convinced? Make sure you have a pencil and paper handy. And remember, there are no right or wrong answers— just revealing ones.

PART 1

Boyfriends, Husbands, Lovers, Others

1. Are You A Giver or A Taker?

There are two kinds of people in the world: those who walk into a room and say "There you are!" and those who say "Here I am!" In other words: givers and takers. The former joyfully open their hearts to others, whereas the latter shine brightest only in the light of their own reflection. And these days, the lights can be seductively blinding.

In the swift and tricky current of our "gimme" millennium, with its focus on the glare of celebrity, it's tough for even the most compassionate soul to sail without occasionally being swept asunder. Who among us can claim to have floated along without swallowing some greed or selfishness?

Here's the hitch: givers can also be takers. If you give-give-give without feeling as if you're getting anything in return, you might have a problem valuing your self-worth, or you're stockpiling resentment. Then again, it could be a motive issue. Anaïs Nin described the delicate balance when she wrote: "I was always ashamed to take. So I gave. It was not a virtue. It was a disguise."

Obviously, there's no simple solution. But our quiz is a good place to start. You'll discover on which side of the give-or-take equation you're standing and whether it feels comfortable.

If you want some tips on how to find a fulfilling balance, give it some thought and *take* our advice.

1. **On the nightly news you hear about a storm ravaging a town about a hundred miles from your home. You call:**
   a. The Red Cross to see how you can help
   b. Friends who live nearby to make sure they're okay
   c. A car service—just in case it starts pouring in your area

2. **Imagine you were writing a novel. You're drawn to which opening line?**
   a. Deeper and deeper, I feel into the well of my own life.
   b. Adoration flowed out of her like ink, staining everything.
   c. Upon a soul absolutely free from thoughts and emotions, even the tiger finds no room to insert its fierce claws.

3. **If you hit the jackpot the first time at a slot machine, you would be more likely to:**
   a. Feed the coins straight back in
   b. Pocket the money and treat your friends to dinner
   c. Play for a while, but be sure to hold onto your original stake

4. **If you witnessed a robbery on the street, you would:**
   a. Try to help
   b. Get out of the way quickly
   c. Run for help

5. **At the end of a particularly good performance at the theater, you:**
   a. Feel constrained and too self-conscious to join in the audience's applause
   b. Applaud energetically
   c. Join in the applause, but feel rather silly

6. **Which virtue do you think is the most important?**
   a. Compassion
   b. Honesty
   c. Obedience

7. **At holiday gatherings you are more likely to be found:**
   a. Enjoying the company
   b. Comparing your appearance to those of other guests
   c. Helping the hostess in the kitchen

8. **What is the statement closest to your personal philosophy?**
   a. Go with the flow.
   b. Stuff happens.
   c. You reap what you sow.

9. **If you met a tedious stranger on a plane who tried to involve you in listening to the story of his life, you would:**
   a. Ruefully reflect that you always meet that sort
   b. Listen with real interest
   c. Politely cut him short and go back to your book

10. **You've said to your boyfriend (at least three hundred times!) that you want something sexy for Christmas. Instead, you get a ten-speed blender! You:**
    a. Threaten to chop him into little bits—only kidding, of course
    b. Gingerly put the gift back in the box and tell him he can make his own malts
    c. Christen the gift by whipping up a potent margarita

11. **You usually root for the:**
    a. Hapless underdog
    b. Powerless victim
    c. Courageous hero

12. **When someone loves you, you:**
    a. Feel uneasy that, as the person gets to know you, the loving will stop
    b. Accept it as your due
    c. Feel glad and do your best to please

13. **When it comes to revealing your past to a new lover, you:**
    a. Share only the information he needs to know so he'll feel comfortable and safe
    b. Explain every scintillating detail—what fun!
    c. Don't tell him unless he asks

14. **A boyfriend asks to borrow $1,000. You:**
    a. Write out a legal IOU with clear terms
    b. Lend it, but feel resentful that he put you on the spot
    c. Tell him it's not a good idea for lovers to lend money to each other, but offer to help him get a loan

15. **On a scale of one to ten, how do you rate your ability to forgive your man?**
    a. Five. It depends upon the situation, but you try to be flexible.
    b. Ten. It doesn't help anyone to hold onto anger.
    c. One. You take no prisoners.

16. **You usually give your lover gifts:**
    a. Only at holidays
    b. On impulse, especially when you see something you know he would love
    c. When you feel guilty or neglectful toward him

13

YOUR SCORE

- Give yourself the following number of points for each answer:

1. a-5, b-3, c-0	9. a-0, b-5, c-3
2. a-0, b-3, c-5	10. a-0, b-3, c-5
3. a-0, b-3, c-5	11. a-5, b-3, c-0
4. a-5, b-0, c-3	12. a-3, b-0, c-5
5. a-0, b-5, c-3	13. a-5, b-0, c-3
6. a-5, b-0, c-3	14. a-5, b-0, c-3
7. a-3, b-0, c-5	15. a-3, b-5, c-0
8. a-5, b-0, c-3	16. a-3, b-5, c-0

60 TO 80 POINTS:
You give it all away!

If you scored this high, you may be generous to a fault. Far from its making you a candidate for sainthood, you could be feeling as if you're not getting enough in return. Inwardly, you're probably seething. And who knows where all this repressed rage is going? Your martyr streak may stem from a poor self-image rather than an abundance of altruism. It's time to take a real look at your motives and figure out what's driving you to doormat status. Meditation, journal writing, yoga, or seeing a therapist are all good ways to dig down into your psyche and mine for genuine gold. Then you can choose to give some of it away without feeling abandoned.

50 TO 79 POINTS:
You're genuinely compassionate.

Your generosity stems from the confidence of knowing and liking yourself: an inner abundance rooted in self-respect. You don't mind doing things for other people because your motives spring from the well of genuine altruism. You usually don't worry about your own hang-ups— nor wonder about the motives of others. Which means, you never feel taken advantage of: you take when you need to. Strolling down this proverbial two-way street of give and take, you're able to see the bigger view.

49 POINTS OR LESS:
You're a taker.

Takers are people who have either been deeply hurt in their lives or always been given everything without having to put too much effort into getting it. Either way, they end up a needy and selfish sponge. Deep down, it probably doesn't feel too great being a taker, either. Ready to let go of "It's all about me"? If so, your first step is to acknowledge where you're at. Then work at forgiving others as well as yourself. It's a big order, but worth it. Famous psychologist Erich Fromm said, "Giving is the highest form of potency." In other words, by letting go, you have everything to gain.

FAST FACT

STUDIES SHOW IF YOU VOLUNTEER, YOU'LL NOT ONLY BE HAPPIER (RESEARCHERS COMPARE THE FEELING OF EUPHORIA MANY VOLUNTEERS EXPERIENCE WITH "RUNNER'S HIGH") BUT YOU'RE 2.5 TIMES MORE LIKELY TO LIVE LONGER THAN THOSE WHO DON'T DO GOOD WORKS.

2. Rate Your Romantic Nature

Part One

1. **Your style of dress could best be described as:**
   a. Soft and feminine
   b. Conservative

2. **You've heard that a friend's marriage has ended. You're most likely first reaction would be:**
   a. Disappointment
   b. Compassion

3. **Of the following film heroes, whose on-screen personality seems more compelling to you?**
   a. Russell Crowe
   b. Tom Hanks

4. **In celebration of your anniversary, you would like your mate to:**
   a. Bring you breakfast in bed
   b. Take the kids out so you can have quiet time

5. **When it comes to dating, you believe:**
   a. A woman should wait to be asked out
   b. It's okay for a woman to ask a man out

6. **When you watch soap operas, you often identify with:**
   a. The hapless heroine who always gets her heart broken
   b. No one

7. **Which of the following seems most true to you?**
   a. You know instantly when you've found Mr. Right.
   b. Love can only grow when it's built on a foundation of respect.

8. **You consider the most loving couple in the public eye to be:**
   a. Angelina and Brad
   b. Michelle and Barack

9. **You would most likely buy your mate boxer shorts made of:**
   a. Silk
   b. Cotton

10. **You daydream:**
    a. Often
    b. Almost never

Part Two

HAVE YOU EVER ...

11. **Sent a homemade Valentine's card?**
    a. Yes.   b. No.

15

12. **Written "I love you" on a foggy mirror?**
    a. Yes.   b. No.

13. **Tried to contact an old flame?**
    a. Yes.   b. No.

14. **Thought your own love story would make a wonderful movie?**
    a. Yes.   b. No.

15. **Prepared an elaborate candlelight dinner for your mate "just because."**
    a. Yes.   b. No.

YOUR SCORE

NOTE: If your answers fall equally between the two categories, read both descriptions, since you share characteristics of both types.

MOSTLY A'S:
You're old-fashioned.

You cherish traditional values: femininity, commitment, family, friendship, and the power of romance. Sentimental and tenderhearted, you surround yourself with beauty. It's easy for you to express loving feelings—from intimate dinners for two to homemade cards and handwritten poems. Romance has always been a priority in your life, and you show it in the way you dress and decorate your home. When you couple your sensitivity with some down-to-earth charm, your romantic nature becomes even more irresistible.

MOSTLY B'S:
You're practical.

You're a warmhearted woman who prefers to get down to brass tacks rather than send out sentimental valentines. Romance, for you, takes on a less traditional expression. You are straightforward, practical, and outspoken. If you care for someone, he knows it; there's nothing coy about your personality. Your honest approach to romance works in your favor—you're most likely to meet a mate who appreciates your directness and recognizes that although you're a realist, you have lots of romance to share.

FAST FACT

WOMEN HAVE AN AVERAGE OF
THREE ROMANTIC FANTASIES A DAY!

3. How Sentimental Are You?

1. You've worn the same perfume for years.
a. True
b. False

2. Strolling along the beach with your partner, you:
a. Pocket as many of the lovely shells as you can carry
b. Pick up the prettiest shell you see to keep as a memento

3. You prefer to spend your holidays:
a. With your extended family
b. With your immediate family

4. When someone asks to see a photo of your family, you:
a. Dig out the mini-album from your purse
b. Open your wallet and proudly display your favorite one

5. What do you remember about your first love?
a. Everything from the color of his eyes to what he wore on your first date.
b. The highlights.

6. You decide to clean out your closet. Sorting through your old clothes, you're more likely to:
a. Hold on to a few of your favorites even though they're a little snug
b. Give away almost everything that no longer fits or is out of style

7. When it comes to classic romantic movies, you prefer such flicks as:
a. *Casablanca* and *Titanic*
b. *Sleepless in Seattle* and *Pretty Woman*

8. For birthdays, you tend to give gifts that are:
a. Extravagant
b. Practical

9. The greeting cards you're more likely to save are:
a. The ones that brought tears to your eyes
b. The ones that made you laugh out loud

10. You've been known to shed a tear or two while watching a television commercial.
a. Yes, quite often.
b. Well … maybe once in a while.

YOUR SCORE

NOTE: If your answers fall equally between the two categories, read both descriptions, since you share characteristics of both types.

MOSTLY A'S:
You're a super softie.

A true romantic, your heart is an open book that you share generously with family and friends. For you, special occasions are priceless, and you can turn even the most ordinary moments into memorable events. It's no wonder people love to gather around you and reminisce! You preserve everything that makes your heart swell—keeping all those wonderful memories within reach!

MOSTLY B'S:
You're a tender touch.

Special moments spent with your family and friends spark your sentimental side and fill you with a deep sense of love. And while some keepsakes will always enjoy a tender spot in your heart, you prefer to relive those moments with loved ones rather than pore over scrapbooks. You tuck away your memories in your heart and clear the way for making new ones.

FAST FACT

WOMEN'S BRAINS ARE WIRED TO RESPOND TO MORE SUBTLE NONVERBAL CUES. THEY USE 20,000 FORMS OF COMMUNICATION A DAY—MEN USE TYPICALLY ONLY 7,000!

4. Rate Your Sex Appeal

Mae West, Marilyn Monroe, and Madonna are known far and wide for it. And you've got it, too. Our revealing quiz will help you discover your personal power to attract the opposite sex!

Part One

1. **When sitting in a chair, you:**
   a. Cross your legs at the knee and rest your hands on your lap
   b. Cross your legs at the ankles and keep your arms on the armrests
   c. Keep your legs close together and cross your arms

2. **If you could spend one day of your life as any animal, you'd be a:**
   a. Thoroughbred racing horse
   b. Siamese cat
   c. Exotic bird

3. **Lately, Mr. Wonderful's eyes have been wandering. To keep them focused, you:**
   a. Threaten to call it quits at the next blink of an eye
   b. Bat your lashes and swoon helplessly with his next caress
   c. Make his eyes pop! You show up on your next date wearing dark glasses, a blond wig, and a slinky chemise.

4. **Which of these subtle sexual signals would you say is your personal calling card?**
   a. Wearing your signature perfume
   b. Wisecracking
   c. Speaking in sensual tones

5. **If you were attracted to a man, you would contact him by:**
   a. Phoning or texting him
   b. E-mailing him
   c. Arranging to run into him by "accident"

6. **When it's time to redecorate your boudoir, you'll buy a:**
   a. Waterbed
   b. Futon, straw mats, and rice-paper screens
   c. Four-poster bed with a lace canopy, puffy throw pillows, and Victorian lamps

7. **Finish this sentence: Men are most attracted to a woman's ...**
   a. Personality
   b. Looks
   c. Mind

8. **When making love with your mate, you are most likely to:**
   a. Lie back and let him take over completely
   b. Take the lead, control the circumstances, and tell him exactly what you want
   c. Join in playful give and take, sharing caresses and fantasies

Part Two

1. **The way to a man's heart is through his senses, not his stomach.**
   Agree_____ Disagree_____

2. I love classical music.

   Agree_____ Disagree_____

3. Pure silk against my bare skin almost
   makes me swoon.

   Agree_____ Disagree_____

4. In romance, a woman should always remain a
   little mysterious.

   Agree_____ Disagree_____

5. I spend lots of my clothing budget on lingerie.

   Agree_____ Disagree_____

YOUR SCORE

- For Part One, give yourself the following num
  ber of points for each answer:

1. a-7, b-5, c-3   5. a-3, b-5, c-7
2. a-5, b-7, c-3   6. a-7, b-3, c-5
3. a-3, b-5, c-7   7. a-5, b-7, c-3
4. a-5, b-3, c-7   8. a-3, b-5, c-7

- For Part Two, give yourself 3 points for each
  statement with which you agree.
- Add the scores from Parts One and Two.

39 POINTS OR LESS:
Demure is one thing—

But you've chosen to take the wallflower approach
when it comes to men. Forget it! It's not that you
don't have what it takes—it's just that you don't
use what you have! It's time to turn yourself into a
tantalizing temptress. Begin by learning the subtle
art of flirting. For shy women like you,

making eye contact is a good beginning. Add a
warm, seductive smile and you'll draw men to you
like bees to honey. Soon enough you'll be singing
the siren's sweet song of success.

40 TO 55 POINTS:
You know how to turn on your sex appeal.

You hesitate to use it. Unfortunately, you consider
it an affront to womanhood. Nonsense! When you
use your innate gifts to attract, you create something beautiful and passionate. There's no need to
feel like a vamp, because you're naturally sensual
and seductive. After all, men use their wiles, too.
You can beguile a guy without entrapping him.
Go ahead and be both bewitching and alluring.
Mesmerize your man with those titillating teases.
Don't wait any longer. Tonight, slip into something
soft and sexy and entice your lover into an evening
of enchantment.

56 POINTS OR MORE:
Coquettish and charming

You have an abundance of sex appeal that men
find both glamorous and captivating. When you
walk into a room, there's an instant response to
your powerful magnetism; men are irresistibly
drawn into your circle. You know how to keep
them interested by listening carefully to their
stories and peppering your own with lively humor
and passionate emotions. You dress with the kind
of flair that makes you appear sensual without
seeming flashy or overexposed. Intuitively, you
know that too much of a good thing gets boring.
You maintain your appeal by adding an element
of mystery.

5. Do You Follow Your Heart?

Part One

Mark the statement that you most agree with.

1. a. Love makes the world go round.
   b. Money makes the world go round …
   but love makes the ride worthwhile.

2. a. I can read a person's true nature in an instant.
   b. It takes time to really know someone.

3. a. I'm an avid collector of mementos and souvenirs.
   b. I clean out my closets and cupboards on
   a regular basis.

4. a. I believe in fate.
   b. I believe we control our own destiny.

5. a. You can change someone through the power of love.
   b. Only we can change ourselves.

Part Two

6. **To win the PTA's support for a project that's close
   to your heart, you'll:**
   a. Appeal to their humanitarian impulses with
   an impassioned speech
   b. Organize and circulate a petition to strengthen
   your cause

7. **The supermarket's gourmet section is promoting
   some mouth-watering (but rather expensive)
   goodies. You're more likely to:**
   a. Treat yourself to the most tempting item
   b. Make due with a few free samples

8. **Which of these accessories says "you"?**
   a. A lovely little vintage purse
   b. A smart-looking bag that carries everything

9. **In your dream biopic, which of these hunks would
   you cast as your leading man?**
   a. Tom Cruise   b. Tom Hanks

10. **Your man could make your heart sing out loud by:**
    a. Offering you a perfect red rose with a graceful flourish
    b. Fixing all the leaky faucets in the house—
    without making you ask even once

YOUR SCORE

NOTE: If your answers fall equally between the
two categories, read both descriptions, since you
share characteristics of both types.

**MOSTLY A'S: YOUR HEART RULES.
A real romantic, you're in love with love.**

You laugh and cry easily, and your reactions are genuine.
However, your sensitivity can be overwhelming. Give
your mind the reins sometimes … but never toughen
up. Your charm is in your generous, loving heart.

**MOSTLY B'S: YOUR MIND RULES.
Passionate about being sensible.**

You listen to your heart but never let it dictate
your actions. But if your grounded approach starts
weighing you down, try trusting emotion … and
see how much sense your feelings make!

6. Which Hollywood Hottie Would Be a Perfect Match?

Research shows the screen idol you adore most may share a key personality trait with you! "We're attracted to movie stars who approach life the same way we do," says relationship expert Jill Spiegel. Who would be *your* romantic ideal? Take this quiz and find out!

1. **You just bought a new TV. What do you do with the box it came in? You:**
   a. Hold on to it in case you need to exchange the TV
   b. Cut it up and use the cardboard around the house
   c. Turn it into a playhouse for the kids
   d. Recycle it

2. **When it comes to fashion, you:**
   a. Find a style that works for you and stick with it!
   b. Favor the classics
   c. Love to experiment
   d. Don't give it much thought

3. **Where would you prefer to live full time?**
   a. A high-rise apartment in a comfortable city.
   b. A farmhouse that you can restore.
   c. A simple beach bungalow on a tropical island.
   d. A new home in a convenient suburb.

4. **Your favorite types of TV shows are:**
   a. Reality, makeover, and decorating and cooking shows
   b. Medical or police/courtroom dramas
   c. Situational or romantic comedies
   d. News, talk shows, and documentaries

5. **You wake up most mornings:**
   a. Eager to get started on your to-do list
   b. Seeking meaning from the dreams you had
   c. Thinking about playing hooky
   d. Hitting the snooze button!

6. **If you were writing a soap opera based on your life, you would call it:**
   a. *The World as It Whirls*
   b. *Day by Day*
   c. *Passions!*
   d. *24/7!*

YOUR SCORE

NOTE: If your answers fall equally between the two categories, read both descriptions, since you share characteristics of both types.

MOSTLY A'S: YOUR PERFECT MATCH IS PIERCE BROSNAN.

Pierce Brosnan has a focused, take-charge personality on screen and off, and like him, "you have a commanding presence," says Spiegel. What else makes you an ideal pair?

- You share strong self-confidence—which drives you to achieve your goals.
- Visionaries like you look to the next step up and don't get bogged down in details.

MOSTLY B'S: YOUR PERFECT MATCH IS BRAD PITT.

What makes Brad Pitt so appealing is a mix of charm and mystery, and you, too, are "a deep thinker who keeps things close to the vest," says Spiegel. Together you ...

- Draw a line between what you share with the world and your private self
- Enjoy spending time alone—and rarely feel lonely!

MOSTLY C'S: YOUR PERFECT MATCH IS RUSSELL CROWE.

Whether he's choosing unique film roles or blazing his own trail in his personal life, Russell Crowe's imagination shines through loud and clear—just like your own, says Spiegel. What else?

- You're both dreamers, always envisioning and creating a more interesting daily existence!
- You'll try anything—once!

MOSTLY D'S: YOUR PERFECT MATCH IS TOM CRUISE.

Tom Cruise wins hearts by always coming through in the end, using logic and persistence to save the day. Like him, "you're a down-to-earth doer who rises to every occasion," says Spiegel. What else?

- You're both fast learners who tune out distractions.
- You keep your cool even in a crisis.

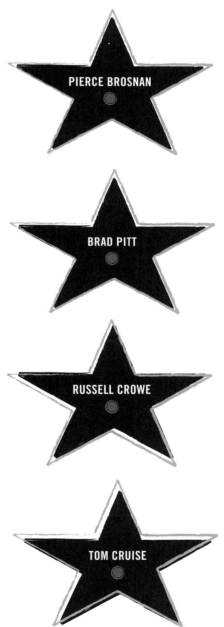

7. Would You Marry for Money?

Are you willing to trade long-lasting romance for a life of riches? Grab a pencil and take this quiz, and see if it's cold, hard cash that really warms your heart!

Part One

1. **If you could create the perfect all-around date, your escort would arrive at the door:**
   a. Carrying a big bouquet of sweetheart roses and a bottle of the best champagne, with a beaming smile that melts your heart
   b. Handing you the key to his brand-new sports car and saying, "It's all yours, baby—now drive me crazy!"
   c. Wrapping you in his Arnold Schwarzenegger–like arms to carry your eager body to the bedroom

2. **If you were to needlepoint a pillow entitled "The Future," which saying would you sew into it?**
   a. Plan carefully and control your own destiny.
   b. Put your faith in the universe and learn the lessons of life.
   c. Open your heart, and happiness will pour forth forever.

3. **Aside from that Disney duck, the Donald who makes you divinely delirious is definitely:**
   a. Don Johnson
   b. Donald Trump
   c. Donald Sutherland

4. **Imagine it: you marry a millionaire without a heart of gold. You would most likely be:**
   a. Miserable. "I'd be living with nothing more than material objects. What kind of existence is that?"
   b. Okay. "After all, I could occupy myself with (almost) anything I desired now that I had the means."
   c. Ecstatic. "I'm sure I could keep myself content with lots of traveling and a wardrobe the world would envy!"

5. **In your high school yearbook, you came closest to being named:**
   a. Most likely to succeed
   b. Best sense of humor
   c. Best looking

6. **To get ahead at work, which of these tactics would you employ?**
   a. Working longer hours.
   b. Buttering up the boss.
   c. Expending more enthusiasm and energy.

7. **If you absolutely had to give up one of the following, you would choose to lose your:**
   a. Bank account. "I was always in the red anyway."
   b. Lover. "He was green with jealousy most of the time."
   c. Job. "Deep down, it makes me blue."

8. **On Sunday morning, the newspaper section you reach for first and follow most closely concerns:**
   a. Society
   b. Fashion
   c. Current events

Part Two

1. **One can't live on love alone.**
   Agree_____ Disagree_____

2. **I usually get what I want.**
   Agree_____ Disagree_____

3. **Frankly, I think romance is just a lot of Hollywood hype.**
   Agree_____ Disagree_____

4. **I prefer luxury living to rustic digs.**
   Agree_____ Disagree

5. **Some people accuse me of being manipulative.**
   Agree_____ Disagree_____

YOUR SCORE

- For Part One, give yourself the following number of points for each answer:

1. a-3, b-7, c-5	5. a-7, b-3, c-5
2. a-5, b-5, c-3	6. a-5, b-7, c-3
3. a-5, b-7, c-3	7. a-3, b-5, c-5
4. a-3, b-5, c-7	8. a-7, b-5, c-3

- For Part Two, give yourself 3 points for each statement with which you agree.

- Add the scores from Parts One and Two.

39 POINTS OR LESS:
An incurable romantic.

You honestly believe you can live on love alone. No wonder you fall for shy, sensitive types who have little or no motivation. We're not knocking love and romance, but you need to be a little more realistic. Someone has to bring home the bread or your relationship will inevitably crumble. Remember when your mom said, "It's just as easy to fall for a rich man as a poor one." She may not have always been right, but perhaps there was more than a morsel of wisdom in her words. Try to keep your eye on a man who at least has the means to make a living and is willing to share the load. In your case, being a fool for love won't pay off.

40 TO 55 POINTS:
You're guided by your sensual side.

But you also look beyond the bedroom for a man who is capable of sharing *all* of life's challenges.

8. How Easy Are You to Live With?

You enjoy working and furthering your career but also expect a fifty-fifty partnership in all aspects of your relationship, including balancing the budget. When it comes to marriage, you want it all: love, responsibility, strength, and compatibility. If you haven't already found him, it may take you a while to meet the man who fits your bill. But the wait is certainly worth it. Your journey together will be filled with both spiritual and material rewards.

56 POINTS OR MORE:
The first time you saw the classic film "How to Marry a Millionaire," you took notes.

With a clear goal in mind, you are determined to marry a man who has big bucks, whether you love him or not. As a result, you turn your nose up at men with less than several million. Cynical and brash, you have no room for romance. The only things that make you happy can be bought—or so you think. We suspect that, although you believe "Diamonds are a girl's best friend," in the end you'll realize that a hard heart eventually hurts. But maybe we're wrong. You're probably banking on it!

Take this quiz and see how much room you can give someone else!

1. **When you make a date and write it down in your diary, you consider it:**
   a. Set in stone
   b. A tentative agreement
   c. Firm, unless there's an unexpected emergency

2. **When you have lots of time to be on your own, you:**
   a. Feel lost, lonely, and depressed
   b. Try to frantically fill in your time with lots of chores, such as shopping
   c. Luxuriate in your own company—soak in the tub, read a novel, surf the Web, or write e-mails

3. **Open your closet door and check out the way your shoes are lined up. They are:**
   a. Like little soldiers in a row, toes pointed straight ahead, heels about-faced
   b. Piled one on top of another—a mountain of multicolored leather
   c. Pretty well organized except for a few pairs of slippers and your everyday sneakers

4. **At the last minute, you're asked to assist with a bake sale for a local charity. You:**
   a. Tell them you haven't got the time—they should have asked earlier
   b. Make no promises, but say you'll see what you can do
   c. Tell them they can count on you to be there

5. **You want to be PTA president but after the votes are counted, you end up in second place—*vice president*. You:**
   a. Refuse the honor—it's president or nothing!
   b. Accept it, but don't take the position as seriously
   c. Start right away on ideas for future meetings

6. **After pouring yourself a piping-hot cup of coffee, you open the refrigerator door and discover you're out of milk. You:**
   a. Close the door and spill the coffee down the drain
   b. Drink it black without enjoying it much
   c. Cover your coffee and run out to the store for milk

7. **Let's say you have a headache. How would you handle it? You:**
   a. Moan and groan and beg your mate to take care of the chores—please
   b. Ask your mate to massage your forehead or bring you a cool compress
   c. Take an aspirin and lie down until the pain passes

YOUR SCORE

- Give yourself 3 points for each "a" answer, 6 points for every "b," and 9 points for each "c."

21 TO 40 POINTS:
Feisty and stubborn

You find it difficult to change directions. You must have things your way, which rules out spontaneity and compromise and makes cohabitation trying. You're also industrious and centered, so stuff gets done. But try to roll with the punches and consider other people's feelings. In fact, let others take the lead once in a while!

41 TO 56 POINTS:
Always on the go

You find it tough to commit to any arrangement—especially a live-in one! You think in terms of "I," not "we," and often overlook the needs of others. But folks put up with you because you're charming and your heart is usually in the right place. The biggest drag? You're too disorganized and distracted to follow through on promises. Make an effort to keep your plans in order: follow lists or a daily diary—or try a chore-sharing chart.

IF YOU SCORED 57 POINTS OR MORE:
Generous and open-minded

You're able to see another's viewpoint without being blinded by your own. You enjoy company, but also have a strong enough sense of self to enjoy the pleasures of solitude. Flexible by nature, you can go with the flow, but you're also willing to let your needs be known when they're important. You always make an effort to keep your commitments firm. That's why living with you must be close to heaven!

9. Do You Keep the Door to Romance Open?

You say you're dying to meet somebody who will sweep you off your feet. But in reality, are you sending signals that push your potential Mr. Right away? Take this telling quiz and see.

Part One

1. **If you wanted to meet a man, which of these moves would you make? You'd:**
   a. Sign on to Match.com, eHarmony or a similar dating service
   b. Tell *everyone* you know
   c. Join a class where you might meet someone

2. **A handsome guy is giving you the eye. You:**
   a. Coyly look away
   b. Flash him a smile
   c. Match his provocative gaze

3. **Which seductive sense would you heighten to warm your man's heart?**
   a. Touch. You'd give him a long, relaxing massage.
   b. Smell. You'd dab on perfume and burn a scented candle.
   c. Sight. You'd rent an X-rated DVD.

4. **Take the closet test. Which colors are most prominent?**
   a. Sophisticated classics (dramatic black and crisp white)
   b. Muted basics (beige and pale gray)
   c. Expressive reds (hot crimson and tender pink)

5. **The man of your dreams is definitely:**
   a. Tall, dark, rich, handsome, and successful
   b. Soft-spoken, a bit shy, and holding a secure (not too demanding) job
   c. Anyone who stirs your heart

6. **An acquaintance wants to set up a blind date between you and her brother's friend. Your first response is:**
   a. "What's wrong with him?"
   b. "Why not?"
   c. "Wait! I need time to think it over."

7. **Be honest: how many hours of each day do you really devote to work or family matters?**
   a. About 8
   b. Between 10 and 12
   c. At least 24!

8. **You dress for:**
   a. Success
   b. Yourself
   c. Others' admiration

Part Two

1. **I admit it. I'm a sentimental fool!**
   Agree_____   Disagree_____

2. **My past is not littered with men who have broken my heart.**
   Agree_____   Disagree_____

3. **As a rule, I pick up on other's subtle signals.**
   Agree_____   Disagree_____

4. **I enjoy walks in the woods, love songs, and romantic movies.**
   Agree_____   Disagree_____

5. **Dinner by candlelight? I don't think there's any other way to dine!**

Agree_____ Disagree_____

YOUR SCORE

For Part One, give yourself the following number of points for each answer:

1. a-5, b-7, c-3
2. a-3, b-5, c-7
3. a-7, b-5, c-3
4. a-5, b-3, c-7
5. a-3, b-5, c-7
6. a-3, b-7, c-5
7. a-7, b-5, c-3
8. a-3, b-5, c-7

- For Part Two, give yourself 3 points for each statement with which you agreed.

- Add your scores from Parts One and Two.

39 POINTS OR LESS:

In the past, you must have suffered a devastating heartbreak and you still haven't healed. As a result, you're not willing to take another chance on love. With your heart shut tight, you feel safe but lonely. It's pointless for you to plunge right back into the arms of another man. You need time, but don't wait too long. When you're ready, take small steps: pay attention to your wardrobe, wear some makeup, read a romance novel, and register with an online dating service. Soon you'll find yourself able to write a new page in your personal love story.

40 TO 55 POINTS:

When it comes to romance, you're usually open and ready. Even though a few of your experiences have been a bit rocky, you're still receptive to new possibilities. But you're not foolhardy. You approach each romantic encounter with a healthy amount of level-headed skepticism. After all, you've learned a lot about men. When you're in a relationship, you're a natural at keeping the sparks alive. You know how important it is to follow the three C's: candlelight, champagne, and cuddling!

56 POINTS OR MORE:

Cupid could be aiming the bow in any direction and, like magic, you'll be standing right there, ready to receive his arrow. Whether you're browsing in the mall or just mowing your lawn— you'll meet a man. You attract romance like a magnet! You have a sixth sense when it comes to sensual pleasures and can turn a man on faster than a car radio. However, you need to be more cautious before falling for every Romeo. Trust your instincts when you think a guy is just pulling your heartstrings. Better to still a love song than have it end on a sour note!

10. Can You Make the First Move?

Do you have what it takes to light a fire under Mr. Right? Grab your pencil and find out just how much gumption you've got!

Part One

1. He passes your desk and you almost pass out with desire. But Mr. Wonderful hasn't even noticed you're breathing. In desperation, you:
   a. Wear a knockout outfit and leave him breathless
   b. Give up. If he hasn't noticed you yet, he never will … or he's dead.
   c. Send an e-mail suggesting you meet after work for a drink. P.S. Make sure it won't spread around the office!

2. Your dream bedroom is:
   a. A field of floral prints and lace, filled with perfume sachets and lit by candles
   b. Comfortable and crisp—with white sheets, pastel linen throw pillows, and antique gaslights
   c. Ultramodern all the way—with stark black and white bedcovers and high-tech lighting

3. At social gatherings, you:
   a. Stick with the old crowd. You have so much catching up to do!
   b. Search for the one-in-a-million man, then make your move
   c. Slowly mingle with the crowd and silently pray a sexy someone will say hello

4. Corny! Corny! Corny! You can't help yourself, you adore:
   a. Reading passionate poetry to your one and only
   b. Watching *Titanic* with your guy's arms wrapped around you

c. Collecting cuddly stuffed animals

5. If the way to a man's heart is through his stomach, the way to a woman's heart is through her:
   a. Body   b. Soul   c. Wallet

6. He says, "Baby, there's something mysterious about you that makes me feel edgy and excited." You say:
   a. "Why don't you come over and uncover my secrets?"
   b. "What you see is what you get."
   c. "Funny, I feel the same way about you."

7. If you could change your name, you would choose:
   a. Ramona   b. Scarlet   c. Penny

8. Before going out on a special date, you:
   a. Get plenty of beauty sleep. You need to feel rested.
   b. Soak in a warm, perfumed bubble bath, then slip into satin or silk underwear. You adore feeling sexy.
   c. Apply makeup meticulously and manicure your nails. You want to be gorgeously groomed.

Part Two

1. Soft lights and mellow music can be sexier than a slinky, low-cut dress.
   Agree_____ Disagree_____

2. I prefer a picnic in the park to dinner at a posh restaurant.
   Agree_____ Disagree_____

3. **Men sometimes need a partner to add the spark before the fires burn.**

   Agree_____ Disagree_____

4. **On the other hand, if one is too obvious, it can smother a guy's passion.**

   Agree_____ Disagree_____

5. **If I met a guy I thought was handsome, I would tell him so.**

   Agree_____ Disagree_____

YOUR SCORE

- For Part One, give yourself the following number of points for each answer:

  1. a-5, b-3, c-7   5. a-5, b-7, c-3
  2. a-7, b-5, c-3   6. a-7, b-3, c-5
  3. a-3, b-7, c-5   7. a-5, b-7, c-3
  4. a-7, b-5, c-3   8. a-3, b-7, c-5

- For Part Two, give yourself 3 points for each statement with which you agreed.

- Add your scores from Parts One and Two.

39 POINTS OR LESS:
Matter-of-fact and practical...

With your two feet firmly on solid ground, romance ranks rather low on your list of priorities. When you meet a man, the match simply feels right, or it doesn't. You have no time (or energy) to waste batting your eyelashes. Everyone dances to his or her own tune, and you prefer a military march to a waltz. That's okay. Maybe you've been hurt in the past, or you're naturally cautious and you feel the need to play it safe. But remember, romance doesn't have to mean heartbreak. It can add just a dollop of desire to an already delicious dessert!

40 TO 55 POINTS:
If a guy makes you feel like floating...

Singing in the rain, and dancing on a cloud, then you're the one to initiate romance. You suggest walks in the country, candlelit dinners, and mellow music. With all this bait, you usually snag your hottie—hook, line, and sinker. But although there are lots of fish in the sea, you're choosy about your catch. So selective, in fact, that you sometimes overlook Mr. Right when he's ripe for romance. Let yourself take that flight of fancy more frequently.

56 POINTS OR MORE:
In love with love...

You're a natural at setting a romantic mood. After you slip into something sexy and dab yourself with perfume, you dim the lights, pour the champagne, and light the fire. Nothing makes you happier than an evening of wine and roses. But your get-up-and-go doesn't stop there! A mover and shaker in business, caring and responsible with your family, you're adept at embracing the best of *all* worlds. Men find this complexity intriguing and are magnetically drawn to your web of whimsy and hard work. Whether it's dancing under the stars with your man or making a stellar presentation to the board, you've earned the title: Queen of Hearts!

11. *What Do Your Fantasies Say about You?*

Do you allow your thoughts to take flight ... or are they rooted in reality? Take this quiz, because what you learn about your fantasy life can be the clue that will help make *all* your dreams come true!

Part One

1. **On a sunny spring day, you walk through a field of yellow daffodils. This image reminds you of:**
    a. The allergy medicine you forgot to take
    b. A poem you once memorized
    c. Golden ballerinas dancing in the sun

2. **The invitation to the costume party reads: "Wear what you want out of life." You've decided to go as:**
    a. A giant diamond wrapped in cellophane decorated with sequins
    b. Yourself, in your dressed-for-success business suit
    c. Mata Hari, in a trench coat and fedora, hot on the trail of adventure

3. **Your favorite fabric is:**
    a. Silk
    b. An easy-breezy synthetic blend
    c. Linen

4. **Let's get personal: while making love, you dwell on:**
    a. Unfinished chores
    b. Your sexy partner
    c. Your favorite movie star

5. **If you were to give your autobiography a title, it would be:**
    a. *Up! Up! Up! My Spirit Soars!*
    b. *How I Have It All—And Still Want More!*
    c. *My Life—Unfolding*

6. **You have a free ticket to travel anywhere on earth. Fill in the blank: Destination...**
    a. Paris
    b. Casablanca
    c. Miami

7. **How much time do you devote each day to daydreaming?**
    a. None!
    b. Half an hour
    c. Half the day

8. **Your ideal job would be:**
    a. A daring trapeze artist
    b. Brad Pitt's private secretary
    c. The head of the United Nations

Part Two

1. **The sky is the limit.**
    Agree_____ Disagree_____

2. **I dream regularly.**
    Agree_____ Disagree_____

3. **If my mate asked me to wear a wig, skimpy slip dress, and high heels to dinner, I'd gladly oblige.**
    Agree_____ Disagree_____

4. **Forget the here and now, I want to know if there's a hereafter!**
    Agree_____ Disagree_____

5. **Halloween is my favorite holiday.**
Agree_____ Disagree_____

YOUR SCORE

- For Part One, give yourself the following number of points for each answer:

1. a-3, b-5, c-7
2. a-5, b-3, c-7
3. a-7, b-3, c-5
4. a-3, b-5, c-7
5. a-7, b-5, c-3
6. a-5, b-7, c-3
7. a-3, b-5, c-7
8. a-7, b-3, c-5

- For Part Two, give yourself 3 points for each statement with which you agreed.

- Add your scores from Parts One and Two.

39 POINTS OR LESS:
You're below sea level.

Unfortunately, you're so down-to-earth, you're below it. Rather than letting your spirit soar and your imagination fly, you prefer to swim in a nest of tangled seaweed. Come up for air! As a child, you were probably the one who had to hold your family together and never allowed yourself to indulge in a fantasy life. But it's never too late. Try devoting several minutes a day to an imaginary scenario. Before long, you'll have the time of your life!

40 TO 55 POINTS:
You're grounded.

Practical and responsible, you make sure that your imagination doesn't run away with itself. However, you do understand the importance of fantasy. As you know, it helps to relieve tension and stress and increases productivity. At the end of a hard day, you often enjoy lying back on the sofa and imagining yourself on a deserted tropical island. This kind of fantasy offers instant peace of mind, helps relax weary muscles, and lowers blood pressure. You've achieved just the right balance between your imagination and your intellect.

56 POINTS OR MORE:
You're in the clouds.

"Earth to *you* …!" Flying high with an imagination that has no limits, you spend most of your time daydreaming. Although it's great to have a healthy fantasy life, you've become too light-headed. Combining a steamy sex life with seductive fantasies is a terrific way to keep lovemaking spicy, but please keep your fantasy life in the bedroom! Don't drift off at work. Your boss may notice that faraway look in your eyes. And watch the road when driving! Touch base more often.

12. Could an Affair Threaten Your Relationship?

You're in it for better or worse, but a dalliance could spell D-I-V-O-R-C-E! Take this quiz and see if your marriage has what it takes to survive.

4. **How would you choose to celebrate your next wedding anniversary?**
   a. What do you mean, "celebrate"? He never even remembers the date!
   b. Stay overnight in the fanciest hotel you can afford and put out the Do Not Disturb sign.
   c. Ask your hubby what he wants to do.

5. **Your neighbor makes a play for your man at a party. What do you do?**
   a. Fawn over *her* husband.
   b. Gently remind your man that he's married.
   c. Threaten to storm out if he returns her advances.

6. **The worst thing about infidelity is:**
   a. What friends and relatives may think
   b. Losing trust in your mate
   c. Knowing someone else was intimate with your spouse

7. **How often do you let your husband know he's the light in your life?**
   a. "Are you kidding?"
   b. At least once a day.
   c. Right after you've kissed and made up.

1. **If a friend told you she spotted your mate sharing lunch with another woman, you would:**
   a. Check his pockets for suspicious receipts
   b. Ask him about it when he comes home from work
   c. Brush it off as just an innocent business meeting

2. **When you see an attractive guy at a party, you:**
   a. Flirt like a fiend, hoping he'll take action
   b. Stand back and merely appreciate the hunk's looks
   c. Fantasize a passionate embrace

3. **If you felt your marriage were seriously shaky, you would:**
   a. Concentrate on what you're getting out of it: a roof over your head, financial support …
   b. See a marriage counselor—immediately!
   c. Wait for the problem to pass

YOUR SCORE

NOTE: If your answers fall equally between the two categories, read both descriptions, since you share characteristics of both types.

MOSTLY A'S:
Your union is already on shaky ground.

What went wrong? Like many couples, you've stopped working on your relationship. You take each other for granted, never compliment each other or set the stage for romance. But all is not lost! Make intimacy a priority *right now*! Open the lines of communication: take time to work through past problems. Once your recognize what brought you together in the first place, you can rekindle the flame.

MOSTLY B'S:
After all this time, the sun still rises and sets on romance.

The key to your marital bliss is understanding. Rather than deny that people are often attracted to the opposite sex, you openly discuss it, then have a good laugh with plenty of loving snuggles. Your man thinks you're sexy and as sweet as can be. He's got it all. He's not likely to look elsewhere and neither are you!

MOSTLY C'S:
You've had some rocky times in your relationship.

Either you've considered having a fling or suspect he might be unfaithful. Rather than call for a divorce lawyer, you've waited for the cloud to pass. Patience is a virtue, but it would be a better idea if you sought professional counseling. Sweeping problems under the rug only means the dust eventually resurfaces. You belong together; now it's time to work on staying that way.

13. What Makes Your Love Special?

1. **For your birthday, your mate will:**
   a. Buy you the one item you want and can really use
   b. Probably give you something completely unexpected and offbeat

2. **When it comes to restaurant reservations, you prefer to:**
   a. Make one at your favorite eatery
   b. Try a new and different place that just opened

3. **Your mate's wardrobe:**
   a. Is basically the same as the day you met
   b. Has changed subtly over the years

4. **You know exactly how your mate's work is going:**
   a. Always
   b. Rarely

5. **During romantic interludes, you'd describe his style as:**
   a. Predictably delightful
   b. Inventive and playful

6. **Your mate's past is:**
   a. An open book he's shared easily with you
   b. A bit of a mystery that's taken some sleuthing to uncover!

7. **He keeps the car radio tuned to:**
   a. His favorite station
   b. Whatever sounds suit his mood in the moment

8. **You arrange vacations by:**
   a. Conferring with each other
   b. Leaving the planning up to one or the other of you

9. **You relatives just invited themselves over for a few days. Before telling your partner the news, you'll:**
   a. Choose the moment carefully
   b. Spring it on him. He can take it.

10. **Has your mate ever played a practical joke on you?**
    a. No
    b. Yes

11. **You find yourself responding to what your husband says with the words "I was just thinking the same!"**
    a. Often
    b. Occasionally

YOUR SCORE

NOTE: if your answers fall equally between the two categories, read both descriptions, since you share characteristics of both types.

MOSTLY A'S:
You know each other by heart!

As close as two peas in an exclusive pod, you and your mate share a strong bond of intimacy. In fact, you can practically read each other's minds and often find yourselves finishing each other's sentences. But if things start feeling a little too routine, let him know by staging your own romantic surprise—send him flowers, mail him a poetic note, or just serve him something new and slightly exotic under flickering candlelight. He'll be sure to get the hint.

14. Understanding Mr. "Write"

MOSTLY B'S:
You still surprise each other.

A sense of spontaneity enhances your relationship, and your love is kept alive with plenty of new experiences. An air of mystery and a flair for fun is your formula for compatibility, so your love can't be rattled by the unexpected. If you should tire of being kept on your toes, try establishing some routines—making Friday "pizza night" or sticking to an annual vacation spot. Who knows? You may enjoy doing the same thing more than you think … together!

FAST FACT

TWO-THIRDS OF US KISS OUR MATE WHEN WE LEAVE THE HOUSE IN THE MORNING.

How your man writes may mean more than *what* he writes!

When you receive a note or letter from your sweetheart, do you linger over every word? You might learn more if you paid just as much attention to his handwriting. According to Sheila Kurtz, a New York graphologist, it's possible to find out whether your favorite man is sensuous, impulsive, vain, open-minded, jealous, or self-confident by simply checking out the way he loops his y's, crosses his t's, and slants his cursive.

Are you ready to look beyond words? Compare your lover's handwriting with these samples.

hello

THE CHARMER

If his handwriting slants all the way to the right, he's an extrovert: emotional, charming, and impulsive. This type might show up with two tickets to the Bahamas and whisk you away. He makes most of his decisions on a whim!

THE PRAGMATIST

Don't expect many surprises from a man who writes straight up and down. He's always objective and calm. If he decides to go on a trip, you can be sure it's after he's read all the brochures and made the reservations weeks in advance.

MR. IMAGINATION

The lower loops of lowercase letters, especially g, j, y, and z, are a clue to his sexuality and creativity. A sweeping, highly exaggerated loop can reveal a terrific imagination, especially in the art of lovemaking

THE INTROVERT

A slant to the left is the sign of a person who has trouble expressing his emotions. He might be outgoing on the surface but secretive about his feelings. If you're looking for someone willing to be swept away, falling in love with this man would mean disaster.

THE LONER

The smaller the loop, the more practical the person. No loop at all can mean your man is a real loner.

A HIGH ACHIEVER

The letter t may tell more about personality than any other letter. The higher the bar on the stem, the higher your man is reaching for success. Add a sweep to the bar, and your guy has lots of enthusiasm, to boot.

THE JEALOUS TYPE

If this handwriting exhibits small loops before initial lowercase letters, he's probably jealous. Keep that in mind next time you think about flirting with a stranger in front of him.

HE'S SO VAIN

Take notice if you see that his lowercase t's and d's are twice the height of the other small letters. That handwriting quirk is an indication of a vain person. He may be good-looking and he may dress like a model, but you'll probably have to fight for some space in front of the mirror!

OPEN-MINDED MAN

The man who writes with open-looped e's is likely to be open-minded and willing to hear your side of the story.

IN CONCLUSION:

"By using handwriting analysis, you can get a deeper understanding of your lover's nature," says Kurtz. "It can alert you to patterns in your love life. When you recognize these clues, you can understand yourself and your partner better." So take note the next time your man leaves one—you may learn the hidden

15. What Kind of Man Do You Attract?

Are you a magnet for Mr. Solid-and-Steady, Mr. Romance, or Mr. Fun? Take this revealing quiz and find out!

1. **The man you'd most likely fall for would say:**
   a. "I never want you to worry about a thing. I'll take care of you."
   b. "You possess the mystery and startling beauty of a shooting star."
   c. "Let's leave everything behind and just run away."

2. **Your male friends have mostly always been:**
   a. Someone to pal around with—to go fishing or to the movie with
   b. Like a big brother—very protective and caring, someone you could bare your soul to
   c. Someone you could fall in love with if you both just let yourselves go

3. **How would you describe your relationship with your father?**
   a. "It's always been strong and loving."
   b. "He was my knight in shining armor."
   c. "He was rarely there when I needed him."

4. **In your opinion, the best place to meet a man is at a:**
   a. Place of worship
   b. Concert or art gallery
   c. Singles event or online dating service

5. **Which of the following most closely describes you?**
   a. Caring and nurturing
   b. Insightful
   c. Happy-go-lucky

6. **If clothes send a message about who you are, what do yours say?**
   a. "I'm straightforward: no muss and frills."
   b. "I'm a hopeless romantic. I love lacy touches and silk against my skin."
   c. "I'm unique. I don't care if colors clash or styles are all mixed up."

7. **Let's take a look at your dating track record. The majority of the men you've gone out with have been:**
   a. Dependable and true to their word
   b. Deep, soulful creatures
   c. Wild risk takers

YOUR SCORE

- Give yourself 3 points for each "a" answer, 6 points for every "b," and 9 points for each "c."

21 TO 33 POINTS:
You attract Mr. Solid-and-Steady.

His conservative exterior may throw you off, but underneath beats the heart of someone who can be your romantic savior. Encourage him and he'll excite you. That he's always there proves his love.

34 TO 51 POINTS:
You attract Mr. Romance.

He'll write you sonnets and bring out your sensual side. But because he's caught up in his emotions, he can miss the big picture. With your help, though, he can be someone to lean on.

52 POINTS OR MORE:
You attract Mr. Fun.

Like a child, he seeks out new experiences and thrills. But that doesn't mean he won't put down roots; a little patience on your end and he'll be keeping his slippers under your bed—for good.

16. The Marriage Clues in Your Valentine's Gift!

If your husband could read your mind, what gift would he bring you this Valentine's Day? Your answer reveals what you love most about marriage, says Marilyn Graman, author of *How to Be Cherished: A Guide to Having the Love You Desire*. So, choose your ideal gift and discover the secret to your marital bliss!

JEWELRY:
You cherish loyalty!

"Just like the unending circle in the rings you exchanged, jewelry symbolizes unbreakable bonds," says Graman. And you're not one to take this steadfastness for granted, just as you're also:

- So committed you'd marry him all over again—studies show 96 percent of women who define their marriages as strong would not only do it again, but in a formal white gown, too!
- Appreciative of how hard you both worked to get where you are—those who like jewelry as gifts know the meaning of money.

CHOCOLATE:
You cherish fun-loving companionship.

Feel like everything is more fun when you do it together? "Chocolate lovers are not only carefree but happiest when they're with those they love," says Graman. So it's no wonder:

- You fall in love with your husband over and over again! Researchers at Chicago's Smell and Taste Research Foundation found that chocolate eaters have elevated levels of the brain chemical phenylalanine, which is linked to that cloud-nine feeling of falling in love.
- You've got the energy to enjoy lots of activities together, since chocolate contains

ingredients—such as caffeine—that keep you going!

LINGERIE:
You cherish cuddle time.

Nothing is better than snuggling on the couch! "This is a woman who holds nothing back in showing her affection," says Graman. Which means:

- You know how to forgive and forget! Affectionate couples kiss and make up rather than hold onto grudges, and marriage counselors say that's the sign of a great marriage!
- You take comfort, and also good health, from the power of touch; sensualists like you get sick less often!

CARD:
You cherish close communication.

"This is a woman who is not only willing to speak her mind but listen with her heart," says Graman. And that give-and-take makes for a strong partnership with your spouse, which shows:

- You're friends as well as lovers—and experts say that since you know how to talk to each other, you're likely to stay together for a lifetime.
- There are no secrets between you—and surveys show that this level of honesty is what spouses want most.

ROSES:
You cherish pure romance.

You're not teenagers anymore, but when you look into his eyes, you still feel like one! "This is a woman who believes it's important to hold onto that magic," says Graman. True romantics like you are also:

- More likely to believe in love at first sight. Surveys show 86 percent of romantics believe in soul mates.
- Drawn to the love stories on soap operas, sitcoms, and dramas. According to the Neilson ratings, true romantics give these shows their highest ratings!

FAST FACT

IN JAPAN, WOMEN GIVE CHOCOLATE TO MEN ON VALENTINE'S DAY!

17. How Much Do You Really Know about Love and Marriage?

Antony and Cleopatra … Romeo and Juliet … Rhett and Scarlett. Love has made the world go 'round throughout history. How wise are you in the ways of romance? Quiz yourself on how much you know about love and marriage—and also find out if you're marriage minded.

1. **King Edward VIII abdicated his throne because he wanted to:**
    a. Divorce his wife
    b. Marry a divorcee
    c. Move in with a model

2. **Which members of the wedding party do not have to stand in the receiving line?**
    a. Mothers
    b. Fathers
    c. Bridesmaids

3. **The theme song for long-married lovebirds George Burns and Gracie Allen was:**
    a. "Love Nest"
    b. "Fly Me to the Moon"
    c. "When the Red, Red Robin Goes Bob-Bob-Bobbin' Along"

4. **When is a thank-you note for the wedding present not necessary?**
    a. When no wedding present was received.
    b. When you absolutely loathe the gift.
    c. When it was given by your husband's ex.

5. **The original purpose of carrying the bride over the threshold was to:**
    a. Keep her gown clean
    b. Prevent her family from forcibly retrieving her
    c. Exhibit the groom's strength and manliness

6. **When the bride wears a dress with a train, the groom should sport:**
    a. A top hat and tails
    b. Anything comfortable
    c. Morning dress for day, white tie for evening affairs

7. **What nerve! Who said, "Falling madly in love with someone is not necessarily the starting point to getting married"?**
    a. Prince Charles
    b. Billy Joel
    c. Oprah Winfrey

8. **For lucky couples celebrating their twentieth anniversary, it is customary to give which gift?**
    a. Lace
    b. Crystal
    c. China

9. **It's legal for a fourteen-year-old to tie the knot in which of these states?**
   a. South Dakota, Vermont, and Virginia
   b. Alabama, Texas, and Utah
   c. Wyoming, North Dakota, and New Mexico

10. **Why do we throw rice at newlyweds?**
    a. To demonstrate a low-cholesterol diet.
    b. To shower them with pure, white thoughts.
    c. To ensure fertility.

YOUR SCORE

The correct answers are:
1. a
2. b
3. a
4. a
5. b
6. c
7. a
8. c
9. b
10. c

- Give yourself 10 points for each correct answer.

30 POINTS OR LESS:
A neophyte in the nuptial and romance department

it's unlikely you'll be making a trip down the aisle soon. Since sentiment is not your strong suit, there's no use saving for a trousseau ... Just yet!

40 TO 60 POINTS:
You have a firm grasp on the traditions behind love and marriage.

It's a sure bet that you've been searching for a while for something old, something new, something borrowed, and something blue. If you haven't already walked down the aisle, you plan to be prepared when the time comes.

70 POINTS OR MORE:
A romance and marriage maven

You could write a comprehensive wedding etiquette book and beat Miss Manners by a mile! In fact, you've probably been to enough wedding parties to keep the entire taffeta industry afloat. There's no doubt: you're a trivia whiz in satin and lace.

18. Are You a Man's Woman?

Some women are like magnets to men. Are you one of the lucky few?

1. **Your date is a hotshot behind the steering wheel. You:**
   a. Scream "Slow down!" until he does
   b. Close your eyes and pray silently for safety
   c. Congratulate him on his keen control

2. **If your man was having a hard time at work, you would:**
   a. Tell him he should just try harder
   b. Insist he talk about it
   c. Give him lots of encouragement to help him ride out the storm

3. **If you were playing a competitive game of Ping-Pong with your partner, you'd:**
   a. Accuse him of cheating so you could increase your score
   b. Let him have an easy victory
   c. Have fun playing—and make him work to win

4. **You prefer wearing:**
   a. Comfortable pants and matching tops
   b. Simple shirtwaist dresses and flat shoes
   c. Short skirts and sheer stockings

5. **Which one of you usually initiates sex?**
   a. "Who remembers? It's been so long!"
   b. You do. You let him know exactly when, where, and what you want.
   c. With your subtle seductive powers, you let him *think* he always does.

6. **You're sitting across from your mate when a pretty woman walks by. He turns to look her over. You:**
   a. Throw a fit
   b. Pretend not to notice
   c. Act a little jealous

7. **You suggest you celebrate your anniversary by going to the:**
   a. Ballet
   b. Best new restaurant in town
   c. Ball game first, then a ritzy hotel with a bottle of champagne

YOUR SCORE

NOTE: If your answers fall equally between the two categories, read both descriptions, since you share characteristics of both types.

MOSTLY A'S:
To everyone else, it seems you don't have a clue as to what makes men tick

But appearances can be deceiving. You know all about them, but your guard is up. Maybe you're hurt or just plain angry about past experiences; thus, you're carrying on your own private war between the sexes. It's time for you to lay down your armor and open your heart. Any man would want you, but first he must get to know the real you. The first step is always the hardest—take a small one today.

MOSTLY B'S:
Men are immediately attracted to your beauty, sex appeal, and charm.

But the tide turns when the relationship deepens. You have trouble stroking your man's ego— and there isn't a man alive who doesn't need his confidence built up. You won't lose your self-respect if you flatter your fellow. His happiness can be contagious. Allow yourself to give in to some of his small demands. Once you make your mate feel as if he's sitting on top of the world, he'll put you on a pedestal.

MOSTLY C'S:
Move over, Angelina!

You're the quintessential man's woman. You can turn a man's head and open his heart, but you never abuse your power. You know how to play the game of love so your partner always feels like a winner (and you know you win, too!). You're sexy, playful, and intelligent. What's more, you're a great listener—and most men find this irresistible. That's why you can work magic on the most reluctant Romeo. It's no wonder that so many men want you both as a lover and as a friend!

Part One

1. **Which of these do you think is most important for a good marriage?**
   a. Good communication
   b. Strong affection

2. **Which quality about your guy do you most admire?**
   a. He really listens.
   b. He can sense what I need without my having to spell it out.

3. **How has this relationship changed you for the better?**
   a. You have become a more considerate person.
   b. You feel your life has more purpose and meaning.

4. **On your first date:**
   a. You talked for hours and hours.
   b. It was pretty much an undeniable physical attraction from first sight.

Part Two

5. **Whenever you have a problem, the first person you talk to is your man.**
   a. True
   b. False

6. **You not only know all your partner's close friends, but you've also met most of his co-workers.**
   a. True
   b. False

7. **You'd rather go to dinner with your guy than see a movie with him.**
   a. True
   b. False

8. **You call each other at least once a day to catch up on news.**
   a. True
   b. False

9. **You can count on him to help with chores.**
   a. True
   b. False

10. **You have no secrets.**
   a. True
   b. False

YOUR SCORE

NOTE: If your answers fall equally between the two categories, read both descriptions, since you share characteristics of both types.

MOSTLY A'S:
Your relationship is built on INTIMATE COMMUNICATION.

There is nothing you wouldn't share with your mate—your heart is an open book! You both believe in the importance of communication, and as a result your marriage thrives. Most decisions are shared, whether it's determining household chores, budget matters, or child-rearing duties. You both love to sit down after dinner and chat about your days. Since you share all your secrets and talk about what's on your mind, your partner is not only your soul mate but also your best buddy.

MOSTLY B'S:
Your relationship is built on PASSIONATE CONNECTION.

For you and your guy, it was probably love at first sight. Something deep inside you two ignited, and the feeling is still going strong. You fully appreciate each other for the unique qualities you possess. Since you both have easygoing natures, you spend less time talking and more time enjoying each other's company. Even if you're just watching television together, it feels great. Love keeps you both feeling warm, cozy, and content.

FAST FACT

WHAT TO WATCH ON TV IS THE MOST HOTLY DEBATED ISSUE BETWEEN COUPLES, AFTER MONEY!

20. How Passionate Are You?

1. **You have a desperate need to satisfy a chocolate craving. You choose a:**
    a. Tootsie Roll   b. Chocolate brownie
    c. Double-dip hot fudge sundae with chunky chocolate chip ice cream

2. **You feel that taxes are too high, so you:**
    a. Get peeved every year around tax time, but write your check anyway
    b. Send letters of complaint to your senator and congressman
    c. Turn them in late! It's your way of protesting!

3. **Most of the men you've been drawn to have been:**
    a. Tender, easygoing, and a little reserved
    b. Playful, charming, and outgoing
    c. Strong-willed, charismatic, and totally sexy

4. **If you wanted to design and stitch your own wardrobe, your first course of action would probably be to:**
    a. Look through pattern books and think of some simple alterations
    b. Spend some time fantasizing about styles and drawing sketches
    c. Buy some unusual fabric and sew a dress that would make Ralph Lauren jealous

5. **A close friend needs your help, but giving it would cause you considerable trouble and expense. You would:**
    a. Give only so much so you won't be inconvenienced
    b. Ask how you can best be of help, then act accordingly
    c. Rush to her aid without having asked and act without any encouragement

6. **If you wanted tonight to go down as the most romantic in history, the most crucial element would be:**
    a. "I don't discuss that kind of thing."
    b. Candlelight, roses, and soft music
    c. High-octane chemical attraction

7. **For you, having two relationships going on at once would be:**
    a. Out of the question. You couldn't possibly give yourself to more than one man at a time.
    b. Confusing. You'd feel emotionally torn.
    c. A delicious luxury, as long as you found both men irresistible

YOUR SCORE

Give yourself 3 points for each "a" answer, 6 points for every "b," and 9 points for each "c."

21 TO 33 POINTS:
Nothing much gets you fired up.

Basically, you keep yourself cool and detached. Fear is keeping you from being enthusiastic about anything. Although playing it safe has its benefits, it's bound to be lonely. Start by sharing your feelings and fears with someone. Once you learn to trust your passion, life will naturally ignite.

34 TO 51 POINTS:
Your passion meter is stuck halfway between hot and cold.

Although you're always eager to get involved in community issues or your career, when it comes to romance, you take a step back. Matters of the heart feel risky; you're less willing to throw yourself wholeheartedly into them. Examine the reasons for your distancing. Let down your guard and allow the same passions that rule other areas of your life to fuel romance.

52 POINTS OR MORE:
Your emotions run high, and that's why you're always burning with passion!

But while this makes life exciting, you sometimes take on more than you can handle. It's wonderful that your heart is so expansive and your enthusiasm so zesty, but you don't want to burn yourself out. Your passion might last longer if you learned to tame it just slightly.

1. **Your idea of a memorable vacation is:**
   a. Returning to the spot where you first met, to relive those special moments
   b. Exploring a new locale with your lover

2. **The place you're most likely to display a photo or your partner is:**
   a. On the bedroom wall
   b. On the living room table

3. **Do you still have all the cards and letters he ever sent you?**
   a. Yes.
   b. You've only kept the ones that are truly special.

4. **You think of your mate:**
   a. At least four times a day
   b. At least two times daily

5. **You'd rather your honey:**
   a. Brought you a dozen roses
   b. Called you out of the blue just to see how your day was going

6. **The one thing you wish you and your mate had more time for is:**
   a. Romantic interludes
   b. Heart-to-heart talks

7. **You're serving dinner to celebrate your anniversary. You make:**
   a. A dish he loves
   b. Something fancy from a new cookbook

8. **The kind of communication you both share is:**
   a. Often unspoken—you can usually guess what he's going to say
   b. Very direct—you both say what's on your mind

9. **You're more likely to tell friends about the time you both:**
   a. Met
   b. Kissed

10. **He could truly touch your heart by:**
    a. Giving you a necklace
    b. Cooking you dinner

YOUR SCORE

NOTE: If your answers fall equally between the two categories, read both descriptions, since you share characteristics of both types.

MOSTLY A'S:
You value memories renewed.

You'll never forget the way your heart soared when you first met your mate, and nothing rekindles that special spark more that reliving your fondest memories. It's no wonder you love to sit with him and pore over old photos. To keep your sentimental heart swelling, reminisce aloud about places you haven't visited and things you haven't done in a while. Since your guy already knows you're a softy, that should be all the reminder he needs to start re-creating those cherished moments of your past.

MOSTLY B'S:
You value day-to-day expressions.

For you, a simple "I love you" can go a long way, because nothing captures your heart more than the daily connections you and your husband share. But although you look forward to the familiar pleasures of having dinner together and cuddling in front of the TV, you also enjoy a few surprises now and then. So keep the flames ablaze by serving an impromptu candlelit dinner or sending him flowers—the new twist on your routine should be the spur he needs to woo you in unexpected ways!

FAST FACT:

THE FIRST THING 58 PERCENT OF MEN DO WHEN THEY COME HOME FROM WORK IS HUG THEIR WIFE!

22. *Will Your Love Last?*

Take this quiz and see if you'll live happily ever after.

Part One

1. **A former flame phones to say he'd like to meet for lunch. Suddenly, you feel that passion return. Without telling your mate, you:**
   a. Meet somewhere secluded and let the heat rise
   b. Douse yourself with cold water and decline the invitation
   c. Agree to meet. But when you arrive, you make it clear your affair is finished—and then leave.

2. **Remember when you met your present man? How were you feeling about yourself back then?**
   a. Fulfilled, joyful, and optimistic about the future—you knew you had finally met your match.
   b. Uncertain but hopeful—he reaffirmed your belief in romance.
   c. Lonely, miserable, and desperate—he literally saved your life.

3. **Complete this sentence, "My man is first and foremost my ..."**
   a. Responsibility
   b. Best friend
   c. Lover

4. **He says yes! You say no! The next step in this scenario is:**
   a. A maybe
   b. A big blowup
   c. Stony silence

5. **It's your birthday. Which of these gifts will your beau be likely to buy for you?**
   a. A kitchen gadget.
   b. Something silky and sexy.
   c. A card.

6. **Your in-laws phone to say they're coming to stay for a week. Your first reaction is to:**
   a. Jump for joy! They're a pleasure to have around.
   b. Sink your face in your pillow—disaster looms
   c. Do your housework—you want everything to be just right!

7. **When it comes to money, you two:**
   a. Argue constantly. He's as tight as a pair of shoes two sizes too small.
   b. Agree in general. However, he's too extravagant when it comes to his hobbies.
   c. Are right on the same track

8. **How often do you make love?**
   a. Every chance you get—you can't get enough.
   b. If you're lucky—and the kids are asleep—once or twice a week.
   c. Who remembers?

Part Two

1. **In an emergency, I contact my mate first.**
   Agree_____   Disagree_____

2. **I can tell my partner anything.**
   Agree_____   Disagree_____

3. **When I'm upset, I let it out right away.**
   Agree_____   Disagree_____

4. **Either he cooks and I wash, or vice versa.**
   Agree_____   Disagree_____

5. **My family thinks my guy is a catch.**
   Agree_____   Disagree_____

YOUR SCORE

For Part One, give yourself the following number of points for each answer:

1. a-3, b-7, c-5   5. a-5, b-7, c-3
2. a-7, b-5, c-3   6. a-7, b-3, c-5
3. a-3, b-7, c-5   7. a-3, b-5, c-7
4. a-7, b-5, c-3   8. a-5, b-7, c-3

- For Part Two, give yourself 3 points for each statement with which you agreed.

- Add your scores from Parts One and Two.

39 POINTS OR LESS:
Your relationship has about as much staying power as an ice-cream cone in the broiling desert sun.

This comes as no news to you, since you're probably miserable in it most of the time. Don't feel guilty: it's nobody's fault. Yes, contemplating life alone is distressing, but with your charm, it should be only a temporary condition. Be brave and either initiate professional counseling or consider a breakup. Once done, you'll breathe a sigh of relief—*several.*

40 TO 55 POINTS:
Your relationship has the potential to endure, but at the moment you're treading on thin ice.

Essentially, you both share many interests and values. Your problem, however, is misdirected anger. If your mate makes you mad, you must learn to voice your disapproval and not stifle or try to sugarcoat it. These negative feelings can crop up in more destructive ways: withholding sex, slamming drawers, bitter comments. Turn to a fresh page in your love story and begin to express your real emotions. Once you do, you and your mate will have a long road ahead to travel—together.

56 POINTS OR MORE:
"Forever" is a weighty word, but when it comes to your relationship, it's the only one that fits.

You two were meant to be together. Every aspect of your personalities is complementary. The key to your healthy love affair? You each allow the other to grow and change without feeling threatened. In fact, you wish nothing more than for your mate to be happy and fulfilled, and he feels the same way about you. If you haven't already married this man, don't wait another minute! Your nuptial knot will stay tied forever.

23. How Much Do You Know about the Birds and the Bees?

You've heard of puppy love, but what do you really know about the mating habits of our four- (or more) footed friends? Take this quiz and learn about courtship in the animal kingdom—you'll be surprised at what you discover!

1. **During mating season, male whales show passion for their adoring mates by:**
   a. Whacking their long fins loudly on the backs of their flirtatious partners
   b. Smooching snout-to-snout
   c. Spouting foam over their favorite female's head

2. **Minks are murderous little creatures except when they:**
   a. Meet their mates
   b. Care for their babies
   c. Have had a good dinner

3. **Those flashy fireflies wink their lights to:**
   a. See more clearly in the dark
   b. Lure enemies away from their young
   c. Signal to fireflies of the opposite sex that they're in the mood for love

4. **After spending seventeen years underground as a nymph, the cicada emerges and lives:**
   a. Seventeen years
   b. One summer
   c. Three to five years (hibernating each winter)

5. **The member of the cat family who leaves the pack in mating season to be alone with his lover is the:**
   a. Tiger
   b. Lion
   c. Cougar

6. **The regal female eagle clearly believes in women's lib, for she insists her mate:**
   a. Share in keeping the nest clean
   b. Take turns incubating the egg
   c. Let her call the shots during courtship

7. **Some say polar bears make overprotective moms because they:**
   a. Cuddle their cubs until the babies grow too big to sit on their mom's lap
   b. Take constant care of their offspring for two years
   c. Refuse to let them play with their brothers and sisters

8. **For most male spiders, courtship is a perilous and complicated procedure because:**
   a. The female often savagely kills her mate
   b. He must perform an intricate dance before lovemaking
   c. Male spiders are naive when it comes to love and sometimes fall into the wrong web

9. **According to mythology, the pattern on the male peacock's tail, which is meant to attract females, was created when:**
   a. Pandora opened the box and bright bird feathers flew out
   b. Narcissus saw his reflection and a peacock stared back
   c. Juno, goddess of marriage, put the eyes of Argus, a one-hundred-eyed monster, on her favorite bird

10. Although a full-grown kangaroo stands taller than a man, the newborn in her pouch is about the size of a:
    a. Big bee
    b. Mouse
    c. Miniature poodle

YOUR SCORE

The correct answers are:

1. a
2. b
3. c
4. b
5. b
6. b
7. b
8. a
9. c
10. a

- Give yourself 10 points for each correct answer.

30 POINTS OR LESS:
You're fascinated by the human condition.

But when it comes to the animal kingdom and their romantic natures, you're a court jester. It may be time for you to cultivate a greater understanding not only of our four-legged friends but of all the creatures on this earth.

40 TO 60 POINTS:
You're crazy about living things, large and small.

Your heart opens wide when it comes to their feelings, and you're especially concerned about animal cruelty. Although you may lack scientific knowledge, your emotional connection, especially when it comes to animal love, is strong.

70 POINTS OR MORE:
You have a thirst for knowledge of the animal world that goes beyond their mating habits.

Perhaps you should consider working with animals. They need our help now.

24. Discover Your Romance Style in Your Favorite Color of Rose!

What woman doesn't dream of receiving a beautiful bouquet of roses from her lover? And the color you'd love best offers clues to your romantic nature! "Color represents emotions and moods—and in roses, that applies to our romantic temperament," explains Leatrice Eiseman, director of the Eiseman Center for Color Information and author of *Colors for Your Every Mood*.

WHITE: You're COMPLICATED.

There's no purer color than white! "As roses, they represent innocence, simplicity, and a calm, quiet approach to romance," says Eiseman. Which means:
You let your actions speak louder than your words, preferring to show—rather than talk about—your feelings.

RED: You're PASSIONATE.

"Research shows red promotes excitement, dynamism, and strong emotions," says Eiseman. People who love this vibrant hue tend to be passionate about love and life, and also:
Love a challenge—especially in romance! Red excites the brain and encourages you to go for it!

LAVENDER: You're MYSTERIOUS.

When it comes to romance, lavender lovers prefer a little intrigue. "You're drawn to subtlety," explains Eiseman. You also:
Know how to tap into your power of intuition to stay connected to those you love, according to research.

YELLOW: You're HAPPY-GO-LUCKY.

"In studies, yellow is associated with optimism and playfulness," says Eiseman. That positive energy not only makes you lucky in love, but you also:
Are great to wake up next to since you start the day happy and full of cheer.

PEACH: You're NURTURING.

"In ancient times, shades of orange—including peach—signaled warmth and devotion in both the real world and the spiritual," says Eiseman. You spread your love generously, and you're:
A natural cuddler, since color-association tests link peach to the warm and fuzzy sense of touch!

PINK: You're ROMANTIC TO THE CORE.

"Softer than red, pink is the favorite of ultrafeminine, sensual types who live for romance," says Eiseman. And if they're your ideal color rose, you're:
A whiz at setting the mood. Marketing studies prove it: fans of the color pink buy more candles, lingerie, and soft music than does anyone else!

FAST FACT

THE WORLD'S LARGEST LIVING ROSEBUSH WAS PLANTED IN TOMBSTONE, ARIZONA, NEARLY THREE CENTURIES AGO! ITS TRUNK IS ALMOST SIX FEET AROUND AND IT HAS, ON AVERAGE, 200,000 BLOSSOMS!

25. Is It "Really" Love?

Does your relationship have what it takes for the two of you to build a life together? Take this test and find out!

1. **You're spending three hours with your guy. How much time will you spend talking?**
   a. Not much. You'll probably watch a movie.
   b. Plenty. You have so much to share.
   c. None. You'll be too busy smooching.

2. **It's been a few days since you last had any time together. You find yourself:**
   a. Thinking about him every once in a while
   b. Letting thoughts of him frequently enter activities
   c. Endlessly fantasizing about him

3. **How far into the future have you looked with your man?**
   a. A few weeks. You're planning a trip together.
   b. A long way down the road. You've talked about getting married and having kids.
   c. Ten minutes—just to decide who's opening the bottle of champagne.

4. **If you had to predict your birthday gift from your man, it would be:**
   a. A nice picture frame or photo album filled with your favorite snapshots
   b. A piece of jewelry
   c. Sexy lingerie

5. **You've made plans for dinner, but now you don't feel well. What is most likely to happen?**
   a. He'll stop by with takeout and you'll watch the tube together.
   b. He'll run over to nurse you back to health.
   c. He'll reschedule the date for when you're feeling better.

6. **Since you met your maybe–Mr. Right, your social circle has:**
   a. Pretty much remained the same
   b. Gotten wider, because now you know his friends and family
   c. Shrunk—you hardly ever see your friends ever since you met him

7. **If you had to describe one aspect that most interests you about your man, it would be his:**
   a. Ambition
   b. Sensitivity
   c. Body

YOUR SCORE

- Give yourself 3 points for each "a" answer, 6 points for every "b," and 9 points for each "c."

21 TO 33 POINTS:
Although you enjoy each other's company, true love—and sparks of passion—appear to be lacking.

Encourage him to engage in deeper conversations. If he still treats you like a buddy, take comfort that you've probably got a friend for life!

34 TO 51 POINTS:
The saying "A match made in heaven" describes the two of you.

You share the same interests, ideals, and goals; you're sexually drawn to him, and it feels natural to talk about your future together.

52 POINTS OR MORE:
You're passionately attracted to your man, but that's it ... for now.

You don't share secrets, friends, or the future. Give this man a chance to be a more active participant in your life. It's the only way to find out if you have more in common. Try spending a date *out* of bed!

26. Take a Trip Down Memory Lane with Our Most Romantic Test!

Just how much do you know about the famous lovebirds who've entertained us on-screen—and off? Take this trivia love test and find out!

1. While tiptoeing through the tulips, they became husband and wife on Johnny Carson's *Tonight Show*:
   a. John Lennon and Yoko Ono
   b. Tiny Tim and Miss Vicki
   c. Tom Hayden and Jane Fonda

2. Which classic Hollywood couple married and divorced, then married and divorced other people, and finally remarried each other? (Their marriage ended only when one of them died.)
   a. Robert Wagner and Natalie Wood
   b. Richard Burton and Elizabeth Taylor
   c. Spencer Tracy and Lauren Bacall

3. Which of these famous Broadway couples were not a husband-and-wife team?
   a. Jessica Tandy and Hume Cronyn
   b. Anne Jackson and Eli Wallach
   c. Betty Comden and Adolph Green

4. When Greer Garson met her future husband, Richard Ney, during the filming of *Mrs. Miniver*, what role was Ney playing?
   a. Her husband
   b. He son
   c. A Nazi soldier

5. Charles Farrell and Janet Gaynor were filmdom's most romantic couple in the '30s. What was their nickname?
   a. The Love Bugs
   b. America's Favorite Lovebirds
   c. Sugarcoated Sweethearts

6. Burt Reynolds has a passion for blondes. Which one did he end up marrying?
   a. Loni Anderson
   b. Dinah Shore
   c. Carol Channing

7. Robert Young and Jane Wyatt lived in matrimonial harmony on the popular '50s TV show:
   a. *My Little Margie*
   b. *Father Knows Best*
   c. *Our Miss Brooks*

8. George and Marian Kerby, frequent visitors to Topper's home, will probably be best known as the longest-married couple in movie history because they:
   a. Were ghosts
   b. Celebrated their golden anniversary
   c. Vowed never to divorce—ever!

9. Oliver Barrett IV said these unforgettable words to Jennifer Cavaleri:
   a. "To be or not to be?—that is the question."
   b. "Love means never having to say you're sorry."
   c. "Frankly, Jenny, I don't give a damn!"

10. Tony and Maria's romance ended in tragedy when he was killed by a rival gang member. Their fatal affair was immortalized in:
    a. *West Side Story*
    b. *Brigadoon*
    c. *South Pacific*

11. **In the classic Disney animated movie, Princess Aurora (widely known as Sleeping Beauty) slept for one hundred years until a handsome prince came along and kissed her awake. What was his name?**
    a. Froggie
    b. Phillip
    c. Prince of Peace

YOUR SCORE

The correct answers are:

1. b
2. a
3. c
4. b
5. b
6. a
7. b
8. a
9. b
10. a
11. b

- Give yourself 10 points for each correct answer.

40 POINTS OR LESS:
You're resistant to romance.

Scientific and practical, you have little place in your reality for romance. As a result, you pay hardly any attention to matters (and affairs) of the heart. If you would only let some more sentiment shine on your soul, you'd learn that love does make the world go round—and there are millions of romantic couples to prove it! With less cynicism, you and that special someone could be one of them!

50 TO 90 POINTS:
You're couple-conscious.

You have a natural affinity to love stories, whether in fantasy, film, or real life. Consequently, you crave romantic movies and sentimental novels the same way a chocoholic yearns for brownies. Like Cupid, you derive pleasure from seeing couples be happy, knowing they can be the balm for a wounded world. Although the greatest love story ever told is probably in your own home, you tend to look toward Hollywood's version. Search your own heart for the real romantic flame.

100 POINTS OR MORE:
You're dynamite on duos.

Call it amour, romance, or LUV, you're hooked! A walking encyclopedia on Eros, you know who's been with whom since Adam and Eve left Eden. Totally fascinated by passion's purpose, you track every romance ever recorded. Your idols range from Romeo and Juliet to Angelina and Brad. You could write *The Book of Love*!

27. How Well Do You Know Your Mate?

Part One

Without much input from your partner, you can usually guess:

1. **What he'll order in a restaurant.**
   a. Yes.
   b. No.

2. **What special something he wants you to give him for Valentine's Day.**
   a. Yes.
   b. No.

3. **The reasons behind his moods.**
   a. Yes.
   b. No.

4. **Where he is at any point during the day.**
   a. Yes.
   b. No.

5. **When he needs some time to himself.**
   a. Yes.
   b. No.

Part Two

6. **You know your husband's social security number.**
   a. True
   b. False

7. **Your mate asks you to buy him a new shirt. You:**
   a. Know exactly what size and style he prefers
   b. Check the styles of shirts in his closet before heading out

8. **While dressing for an evening out, you're more likely to:**
   a. Slip into the dress that makes his eyes light up
   b. Hold up a few outfits to gauge his reaction

9. **If he were planning a surprise party for you, would he be able to keep it a secret?**
   a. No. You'd probably pick up his unintentional clues.
   b. Yes. He'd put on his best poker face— and you'd never suspect!

10. **The details of your mate's childhood are:**
    a. As familiar to you as your own
    b. Sketchy. He doesn't talk about it much.

11. **The one thing that you can count on when the Sunday paper appears is:**
    a. Having to wait to read certain sections— your mate always grabs them first!
    b. Catching up on the latest news with your man

YOUR SCORE

NOTE: If your answers fall equally between the two categories, read both descriptions, since you share characteristics of both types.

MOSTLY A'S:
You know him as well as you know yourself.

You know him backward and forward, from his likes and dislikes to the memories of his youth. He's an open book—and every page is a pleasure to read. You find every aspect of his life interesting, and all the little details are part of why you love him!

MOSTLY B'S:
He's a lovable mystery man.

You may wish you knew more about him—and time will no doubt tell all—but your mate can't be pegged yet. Your confident that his heart is yours, and one thing you do know and love about him is that he's never boring!

When it comes to romance, do you see everything through a rose-colored fog? Take this quiz and become a winner at the game of love!

Part One

1. **You get a news flash through the grapevine that the dashing man you've been dating has a reputation as a rascal and a rat. You say:**
    a. "So long, Charlie—have a nice life!"
    b. "So, I'll just take it slow and easy and see what happens."
    c. "So what? He'll be different with me."

2. **If you were on the hunt for mate material, you think the most compatible guy could be found:**
    a. Browsing through a bookstore
    b. Catching rays on a sunny beach
    c. Working by your side

3. **A guy who cheats on his wife is probably:**
    a. A hopeless romantic
    b. Misunderstood and likely trapped in a miserable marriage
    c. A cad with an overactive sex drive and an underactive sense of morality

4. **How long does it take to mend your broken heart?**
    a. A few months, then you begin to see the light
    b. A lifetime
    c. A couple of painful years

5. **You can best tell the character of a man by:**
    a. The car he drives
    b. The care he shows
    c. The company he keeps

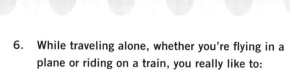

6. **While traveling alone, whether you're flying in a plane or riding on a train, you really like to:**
   a. Read a steamy romance novel
   b. Fantasize about love on the run
   c. Start a conversation with a handsome stranger seated beside you

7. **The man waiting behind you in line casually asks, "Have we met before?" Your first reaction is to:**
   a. Take a good look at him and politely try to recall whether the two of you ever met
   b. Snub him. He's got to be kidding—that line is as old as Moses.
   c. Smile your best smile

8. **If your mate Is acting crabby, you:**
   a. Begin to wonder if it's somehow your fault
   b. Ask him what's wrong
   c. Threaten to walk away if he doesn't snap out of it and start acting human

Part Two:

1. **I would hesitate to enter a relationship thinking I could change a man.**
   Agree_____ Disagree_____

2. **A good relationship requires hard work and compromise.**
   Agree_____ Disagree_____

3. **I realize the Hollywood version of romance is unrealistic.**
   Agree_____ Disagree_____

4. **Most women end up falling in love with men similar to their fathers.**
   Agree_____ Disagree_____

5. **It takes time for lasting love to grow.**
   Agree_____ Disagree_____

YOUR SCORE

Part One

For Part One, give yourself the following number of points for each answer.

1. a-5, b-7, c-3   5. a-3, b-7, c-5
2. a-5, b-3, c-7   6. a-5, b-3, c-7
3. a-3, b-5, c-7   7. a-7, b-5, c-3
4. a-7, b-3, c-5   8. a-3, b-7, c-5

Part Two

- For Part Two, give yourself 3 points for each statement with which you agree.

- Add the scores from Parts One and Two.

39 POINTS OR LESS:
You're usually quite intelligent and levelheaded...

But when it comes to love, you're as daffy as a duck stuck in mud. Reckless and rash, you fall for every Romeo on the road of life. It's time to put the brakes on and drive through the tunnel of love with a little more caution! Learn to read the signals of a hopeless affair. If he says he doesn't want to commit—believe him; he means it! What's more, the chances of changing a cad are a million to one, maybe more. Re-calculate the odds by choosing a different sort of man as your mate. Good looks aren't everything. An ordinary Joe may be just what your foolish heart needs.

40 TO 55 POINTS:
A bit eccentric in everything you do...

It's no surprise you sometimes become less than sensible when it comes to satisfying your sensual appetite. As long as you're not hurt, it's all right to occasionally be a bit reckless in matters of the heart. The good news? You usually know when to call it quits. Although a couple of guys you've known have turned out to be apes, a man has yet to make a monkey out of you. But you should probably exercise a bit more discretion when accepting dates. Learn to use your head as well as your sentimental heart, when looking for Mr. Right.

56 POINTS OR MORE:
Methodical and down-to-earth...

You're nobody's fool. Wise in the ways of romance, you've avoided the pain of a broken heart. Although we commend your sensible outlook, by always being on guard you've missed some golden opportunities. Sometimes you tend to shield yourself from life's challenges. Keep your eyes wide open, but take the plunge when the sea of love feels warm and inviting. There are plenty of fish out there. Get ready to fall hook, line and sinker for that special one.

Men—can't live with 'em, can't live without 'em! But how much do you really know about them? Take this quiz and find out!

1. **You have good news—and bad news. Which should you tell him first?**
    a. Hit him with the happy news first—men like to be let down easy.
    b. Get the worst over at the beginning—boys are brave.
    c. Keep the bad news to yourself—mum's the word.

2. **When men are asked whether they would marry the same spouse again, 90 percent said:**
    a. Yes!
    b. Never!
    c. Maybe.

3. **More than a decade ago, on an average day, only 225 Americans got their noses fixed. How many of these snout-shorteners were men?**
    a. 56
    b. 112
    c. 30

4. **Guys whistle when they see a sexy lady walk by. Which part of her anatomy first catches their eyes?**
    a. Legs
    b. Chest
    c. Face

5. **They insist they help around the house, but how much time do men really spend cooking each day?**
    a. One hour
    b. 15 minutes
    c. 35 minutes

6. The way most men come clean is to:
   a. Bathe
   b. Shower
   c. Bathe, then shower

7. The average guy stands about:
   a. 6 foot 2
   b. 5 foot 11
   c. 5 foot 9

8. Men are most intimidated by a woman who is:
   a. Incredibly gorgeous
   b. Extremely intelligent
   c. Really rich

9. You really love your man's mane. But after his fortieth birthday, there's a ___ chance he'll begin balding.
   a. 10 percent
   b. 60 percent
   c. 25 percent

10. He claims to be an insatiable Romeo, but how often do most men really *want* sex?
   a. Daily
   b. Weekly
   c. Every other day

YOUR SCORE

The correct answers are:

1. b
2. a
3. a
4. c
5. b

6. b
7. c
8. a
9. b
10. c

- Give yourself 10 points for each correct answer.

30 POINTS OR LESS:
Men are a mystery to you!

Since you have so little knowledge when it comes to the opposite sex, you're continually surprised. May we suggest that you try to understand the man in your life a little more and meet him halfway? You have a lot to learn!

40 TO 60 POINTS:
You're mixed up about men.

When it comes to statistical information, you're right on target. However, their emotional needs and romantic desires leave you absolutely baffled at times. Perhaps if you were more honest with our own feelings, those of the opposite sex wouldn't remain so vague.

70 POINTS OR MORE:
You're mad about men.

You know men better than they know themselves. And you're crazy about 'em! As a result of your smarts, guys buzz around you like bees around nectar.

30. How Easily Are You Turned On?

When pleasure comes a-calling, do you allow all your senses to take in the message? Try our revealing quiz ... and get in touch with yourself!

Part One

1. **Which of these skin sensations sounds the most scintillating?**
   a. Massaging your entire body with scented oils.
   b. Jumping into a freezing lake after unwinding in a steamy sauna.
   c. Sinking into sun-baked sand on a deserted beach.

2. **"He was a mysterious stranger—with rippling muscles, auburn hair that danced in the light, and a seductive all-man scent that lingered after he'd left." If you met this mysterious stranger, what do you imagine would most turn you on about him?**
   a. His hair
   b. His scent
   c. His physique

3. **You prefer to quench your thirst with:**
   a. A soft drink, preferably cola
   b. Ice-cold beer
   c. Exotic fruit juice

4. **If you could add on any room to your house, you would make it a:**
   a. Greenhouse—with lush roses and orchids growing all year round.
   b. Giant bathroom—complete with an enormous bathtub, steam room, and Jacuzzi.
   c. Gym—with weights, treadmill, and stationary bike.

5. **In dreams of desire, your lover showers you with:**
   a. Sweet caresses, gentle kisses, and lovely black lace lingerie
   b. Theater tickets and fancy dinners
   c. French perfume, flowers, champagne, and chocolates

6. **For exercise, you prefer:**
   a. Swimming in cool, refreshing water
   b. A few sets of tennis with a well-matched partner
   c. A waterfall rushing down the mountainside

7. **Would you rather have your skin stroked with:**
   a. A feather
   b. A soft silk cloth
   c. Your lover's lips

8. **When buying fabric for your bedcovers, you choose:**
   a. Miracle blends. "Wow! They never need ironing!"
   b. Silk. "Hmmmm! It's an extravagance, but I'm worth it!"
   c. Natural cotton or linen. "Ahhhh! I love the feel—so crisp and cool."

Part Two

1. **I love how sweet the earth smells after a summer rain.**
   Agree_____ Disagree_____

2. **I can feel a cold coming on days before I get the sniffles.**
   Agree_____ Disagree_____

3. **When the mind is relaxed, the body unwinds.**
   Agree_____ Disagree_____

4. I'd rather feel my lover's lips against mine than hear him speak words of endearment.
   Agree_____ Disagree_____

5. Certain smells, sweet or not so, bring me back to my childhood.
   Agree_____ Disagree_____

YOUR SCORE

For Part One, give yourself the following number of points for each answer:

1. a-7, b-2, c-5   5. a-7, b-2, c-5
2. a-5, b-7, c-2   6. a-7, b-2, c-5
3. a-2, b-5, c-7   7. a-5, b-2, c-7
4. a-5, b-7, c-2   8. a-2, b-7, c-5

- For Part Two, give yourself 3 points for each statement with which you agree. Add the scores from Parts One and Two.

39 POINTS OR LESS:
Although you don't exactly wear a suit of armor, luxury and physical pleasure are not tops on your priority list.

You'd rather work hard than pamper yourself. In fact, you think soaking in a tub of fragrant bubbles is a waste of time. Although your dedication to practicality is commendable, trust us: a little luxury goes a long way toward relieving stress and raising sexual desire. And nobody needs to relax more than you! Dedicate just thirty minutes a day to some self-indulgence: read the paper in bed, sit in front of the fire, just cuddle with your honey, or simply watch the birds fly by. Before long, you'll open to your sensual self!

40 TO 55 POINTS:
You have a genuine appreciation for pleasure.

Whether it's the touch of a cuddly kitten, the squeal of a young child's laugh, the deliciously rich taste of chocolate, or the touch of your lover's hand on yours—you love what life has to offer. Just the feel of a warm breeze against your bare skin makes you giddy with delight. Men find your sensitivity exciting and want to join in your zest for life. The only time you set limits is when it comes to money. Conscious of your budget, you never indulge in expensive luxuries, such as furs, baubles, or thousand-count sheets (although you would love it!). With this feet-on-the-ground attitude, you'll always bask in the sunlight, soaking up every ray with sheer sensual pleasure!

56 POINTS OR MORE:
Your senses are your keys to life.

Like the heroine in "The Princess and the Pea," to be happy you need to be utterly comfortable. For you, that means symphonies, sleeping on silk, soaking in scented bathwater, a six-course gourmet meal—and your man all over you! You revel in luxury and loving, and no matter what the cost, monetarily and emotionally, you desire it all! Self-indulgent (just a bit), you tend to crave every creature comfort imaginable. You love the feel of velvet and the exquisite beauty of roses. An artist of sensual pleasures, you're a romantic who is driven by desire and satisfied by sex!

31. Who's Your Fantasy Man?

Married or single, we've all had harmless daydreams about being swept off our feet by one of Hollywood's leading men. "The one you fantasize about can be quite telling," says Sherry Amatenstein, author of *The Q&A Dating Book: Answers to the Most Intimate Questions about Love and Romantic Relationships*. "We're attracted to celebrities who—on-screen and off—appear to have the qualities we value most in a real man," she adds. So choose your Hollywood fantasy hunk, and learn what you most value in a real-life lover!

WILL SMITH:
You like to laugh!

If Will Smith brings a dreamy smile to your face, "you believe a great sense of humor and a playful attitude are essentials for a happy relationship," says Amatenstein. You like a guy who knows how to have fun just like Will. The paparazzi are always snapping shots of Will's clowning around with his kids!

TOM CRUISE:
You like a family man.

Despite his hunky glamour, Tom Cruise is devoted to his wife and children. And he tries to stay out of the Hollywood glamour loop as much as possible—focusing instead on his deeper calling. "If you're turned on by Tom, what you value most in a man is loyalty to family; you want a traditional provider who will be in charge of making the big decisions—someone you can really count on," says Amatenstein.

GEORGE CLOONEY:
You like a charmer.

Other women might not miss it quite as much if it wanes, but you need romance. "Your priority is passion," says Amatenstein. "And your real-life dream guy won't let the two of you settle into ho-hum companionship. He'll keep the spark alive!" she says.

BRAD PITT:
You like them boyish.

Considered one of the sexiest stars around, Brad Pitt has an endearing side—vulnerable and boyish—that wins fans. "If Pitt's your dream date," says Amatenstein, "you love making a fuss over your man." And his appreciative attitude keeps your relationship feeling fresh and new, even when you're dealing with day-to-day family hassles.

32. Does Sensuality Rule Your Romance?

1. In the early stages of a love affair, you're most likely to feel:

a. Like you're on a roller coaster, with marvelous ups and heart-stopping downs

b. Buoyant, cheerful, and wonderfully alive!

c. As though you can't get enough cuddle time

2. Which of these things would you most prefer as a love offering?

a. A gift certificate from a fancy department store

b. Long-stemmed roses

c. Silk lingerie

3. Which qualities do you find most attractive in a man?

a. Good brains, a good job, and good character

b. Charm, great looks, and lots of charisma

c. That mysterious, indefinable thing known only as chemistry

4. How would you rate your dance fever?

a. Cool. You don't have much interest in boogying, but you will dance every now and then.

b. Warm. You like it mainly because it gives you an opportunity to be close to your man.

c. Hot. You do it whenever the beat of the music moves you!

5. Which do you enjoy most—giving or receiving massages?

a. Neither. It makes you feel a little uneasy and self-conscious.

b. Giving. You enjoy being in control and being able to regulate your partner's reactions.

c. Both. It feels just as good to stroke your partner's back as it does when he strokes yours.

6. For a walk along the beach on a summer evening, you'd wear:

a. A pair of shorts and a tank top

b. A shift with spaghetti straps

c. A flowing cotton skirt and halter top

7. The scent you most love to wear is:

a. The clean freshness of baby powder

b. An extravagant French perfume

c. The earthy aroma of musk or patchouli

YOUR SCORE

Give yourself 3 points for each "a" answer; 6 points for every "b," and 9 points for each "c."

21 TO 33 POINTS:
You're not a very sensual person.

You're athletic and appreciate the outdoors more as a challenge than a connection to nature—and your relationship is ruled more by companionship than passion. Often, you're too preoccupied with your own thoughts to notice the scent of fresh flowers or the way your guy breathes warmly on your neck. Girl! Wake up and smell the roses! Your senses are gateways to great pleasure. Use them!!!

34 TO 51 POINTS:
You always appreciate powerful sensations.

Whether it's the aroma of hot coffee, the taste of a fine meal, or your lover's breath on your neck, you delight in living luxuriously but can also enjoy roughing it out in the country—of course under the covers with your man! Everything from warm baths together to walks along the beach arm in arm, easily bring you to a boiling passion.

52 POINTS OR MORE:
You are a true sensualist.

Every one of your senses is highly developed. You love the smell of lavender, the tender touch of a kiss, beautiful sunsets, the ringing of church bells, and the taste of gourmet delicacies. You savor every sensual aspect of life with gusto—and nothing makes you melt more (yes, even more than chocolate!) than the caress of your lover's hands. How lucky you are!

33. Which of These '90s Television Characters Made Your Heart Beat Faster?

We all loved those '90s kind of handsome hunks on our favorite television shows—but did you know that the TV character you'd most like to find sitting next to you on the sofa reveals a lot about your romantic nature? *It's true*! "Our attraction to a particular character is deeply rooted in the traits we value most in ourselves and in our real-life relationships," says Barbara DeAngelis, PhD, author of *What Women Want Men to Know*.

SAM SEABORN FROM *THE WEST WING*:
You're a perfectionist!

What one word describes Sam best? Smooth! This Beltway insider navigates life's ups and downs looking sure, suave, and put together. "You're attracted to Sam because, just like you, he strives for perfection," says DeAngelis. You work hard to juggle your job, family, and home, and it shows: your boss admires you, your kids are always prepared, and your parties are the envy of the neighborhood! But remember: Sam's just a TV character, and no one can be perfect all the time. So when the pressure gets to be too much, put your feet up and relax with your honey—you both deserve it!

BOBBY DONNELL FROM *THE PRACTICE*:
You're an open book!

How many times have you seen sensitive lead lawyer Bobby Donnell call someone into his office and have a private heart-to-heart? "Bobby loves to share his opinions and listen to those of others, and if he's your heartthrob, chances are you put communication at the top of your list," says DeAngelis. Never one to bury your feelings, you believe in getting things out in the open! You know there's almost nothing that can't be solved by shedding the light of day on it—and that's why tough problems—even difficulties in your relationship—are resolved with your special brand of open-hearted honesty!

LUKA KOVAC FROM *ER*:
You're a dyed-in-the-wool romantic!

The not-so-lucky Luka has been through tough times—but it's only made him more tenderhearted. If you were attracted to him, "you're also a romantic, who has a sense of caring and values her relationships with loved ones," says DeAngelis. A soft touch, you can't ignore a crying child, a friend in need, or the tug of your heartstrings when your guy looks at you the way he did when you were first dating!

RICK SAMMLER FROM *ONCE AND AGAIN*:
You're rock steady!

"Odds are you're not just attracted to Rick's handsome face, but to his steady temperament instead. "It matches your own, and it's what you probably admire in your husband," says DeAngelis. Preferring old-fashioned values over wild flights of fancy, you know that a loving family, a comfortable home, and a satisfying job are some of life's greatest joys!

34. What's the Secret to Your Attraction?

Part One

1. **My closet is filled with trendy styles and bright prints.**
   a. Yes.
   b. No.

2. **I'm always one of the first people out on the dance floor.**
   a. Yes.
   b. No.

3. **I'm naturally talkative and often take the lead in group conversations.**
   a. Yes.
   b. No.

4. **People always notice and compliment my perfume.**
   a. Yes.
   b. No.

5. **I like to try out new hairstyles.**
   a. Yes.
   b. No.

6. **If a magician asked for volunteers from the audience, I would raise my hand instantly.**
   a. Yes.
   b. No.

7. **I have lots of pictures of myself and my family around my home.**
   a. Yes.
   b. No.

8. **Cut my makeup routine short if I'm running a few minutes late? Never!**
   a. Yes.
   b. No.

9. **No one ever has to ask for me to speak up—my voice tends to carry.**
   a. Yes.
   b. No.

Part Two

10. **When you walk into a crowded room, you:**
    a. Walk over to a group of people and introduce yourself to those you don't know
    b. See someone you know and start a conversation

11. **At family gatherings, when the camera comes out, you:**
    a. Smile
    b. Offer to take a picture of the whole gang

12. **Your stride can best be described as:**
    a. Sure-footed
    b. Easy and graceful

13. **If you were remodeling your bedroom, you would paint the walls:**
    a. Varying shades of rich rose
    b. Neutral with a clear white trim

14. **If you could buy any car you wanted regardless of price, you would choose a:**
    a. Ferrari
    b. Lexus

YOUR SCORE

NOTE: If your answers fall equally between the two categories, read both descriptions, since you share characteristics of both types.

MOSTLY A'S:
You're naturally radiant.

You exude a stunning combination of confidence and energy that shines outward for all the world to admire. Men want to be within your sphere to reap the benefits of your positive vibrations. Your laughter and enthusiasm and eagerness to join the fun is a turn-on. Who can resist you? It's no wonder you're at the top of so many guest lists—and the woman who can make any man's heart skip a beat. You're a shining star that can brighten any man's life!

MOSTLY B'S:
You're a hidden jewel.

You possess a deep inner beauty that brings out the best in the man you love. You're a compassionate person who truly cares for your guy, and your spirit acts as a magnet to draw him into your sphere. Your subdued style radiates a quiet confidence he admires. It's no wonder even casual acquaintances think you're extra special. Since your light shines bright, it will always be the center of his life.

FAST FACT

DO YOU KNOW 70 PERCENT OF US NEVER LEAVE THE HOUSE WITHOUT PUTTING ON SOME JEWELRY?

PART 2

Friends, Family, Colleagues, and Confidants

1. What Kind of Friend Are You?

1. **While lunching with a friend, you sense something is bothering her. So you say:**
   a. "You seem upset. If you need anything, I'm here for you."
   b. "Friends share everything—please tell me what's going on."

2. **A critical comment from your boss drives you to tears. You comfort yourself by:**
   a. Pouring your heart out to a sympathetic coworker
   b. Calling your best friend immediately

3. **What do you hide from your closest friends?**
   a. Intimate secrets. There are some things you just don't feel comfortable sharing.
   b. Absolutely nothing.

4. **A dear friend has just moved across the country. How often will you talk to her in the next few months?**
   a. At least every few weeks. You'll want to keep in touch.
   b. As often as you have something to share with her—probably once a week or more.

5. **Yesterday, your friend made an unflattering remark about your new hairstyle. Today, she apologizes profusely. Your response?**
   a. "It's nothing. Don't worry about it at all."
   b. "I was pretty hurt—but, of course, I accept your apology."

6. **Two of your friends just don't get along with each other. So you:**
   a. See them separately
   b. Try to find ways to help them overcome their differences

7. **On the night of a pal's party, you're the one who can be counted on to:**
   a. Pop into the kitchen once or twice and offer to help serve or tidy up
   b. Arrive early, help set up, and continue to cohostess throughout the evening

8. **Your friend phones as you and your husband are watching your favorite TV show. You:**
   a. Tell her you'll call back when the show's over
   b. Take the phone into the next room to chat

9. **At a party where you know only one other person, you:**
   a. Greet your pal, chat a bit, then mingle
   b. Stick close to your friend all night, meeting other guests as a duo

YOUR SCORE

NOTE: If your answers fall equally between the two categories, read both descriptions, since you share characteristics of both types.

MOSTLY A'S:
You're at ease.

You take a loving but relaxed approach to friendship, putting the emphasis on quality, not quantity of time spent with your pals. Reliable but never too clingy, you value your own privacy and respect that of others. Family and friends admire your independent spirit, cherishing precious moments spent with you all the more because of it. No wonder you're so popular with everyone.

MOSTLY B'S:
You're high intensity.

You're serious about friendship, offering absolute loyalty and expecting the same in return. An expert secret-keeper, you rarely divulge details friends share in confidence. You're always there to lend a helping hand or a shoulder to cry on. Sometimes you may feel overburdened, but take heart: every last bit of kindness you show will be returned to you tenfold.

FAST FACT

STUDIES HAVE SHOWN THAT PEOPLE WHO MAINTAIN AT LEAST ONE VERY CLOSE FRIENDSHIP TEND TO HAVE FEWER ILLNESSES, STRONGER IMMUNE SYSTEMS, AND LOWER STRESS LEVELS.

2. The Friendship Clues in the "Friend" You Miss Most

Season after season, we wondered if Ross and Rachel would get back together, if Joey would make it as an actor, if Monica and Chandler would have a family, and if Phoebe would find love. Now that *Friends* has ended, who do you miss most? "The one you found hardest to say good-bye to offers clues about what makes your friendships strong," says nationally known psychologist Karen McCallum. So ...

IF YOU MISS MONICA:
You're a creative dynamo.

"Women who are drawn to Monica's take-charge, domestic diva personality tend to be imaginative souls who are so busy with whipping up new creations and ideas that they rely on their friends to help them mind mundane day-to-day details," say McCallum. So it's no surprise that:

- You treat your home like an art project.
- You love to figure out how stuff works—then invent a better solution.

IF YOU MISS RACHEL:
You're practical.

"Contrary to popular belief, women who adore Rachel are actually no-nonsense types who stress simple, traditional values in their own lives, but are amused—and intrigued—by the glamorous fun of fashion-conscious urban friends," says McCallum. Which is why:

- You're loyal to the same brands and products your mother used.
- You're not impressed with fads or trends, but value the tried-and-true!

IF YOU MISS JOEY:
You're a deep thinker.

"Who better than Joey, with his childlike innocence and youthful spirit, to help intelligent types like you—who are always contemplating life's mysteries—tap into that carefree, fun-loving child within?" says McCallum. What else?

- Your favorite pastime is reading or working on puzzles—and you probably own more books than anyone you know!
- You tell it like you see it, but you never judge—which is why research shows you experience 70 percent less stress.

IF YOU MISS PHOEBE:
You're a go-getter!

"You're always on the run and chasing some new goal or challenge—that's why women who are drawn to Phoebe rely on stress-proof friends like her to help them relax and unwind," says McCallum. It's no wonder, then, that:

- You're never late—and studies show planners who stick to their schedules are more likely to finish what they start!
- Your attention to detail is how you make very get-together a picture-perfect event!

IF YOU MISS ROSS:
You're a free spirit!

"Ross's pals know they can count on him to solve problems—which is just what you, who hates to be tied down, seek in a friend," says McCallum. This means:

- You're guided more often by intuition than by intellect.
- You turn daily life into an adventure, exploring every new shop or eatery in town!

IF YOU MISS CHANDLER:
You're the backbone of your family!

Chandler won Monica's heart with his sense of humor, and if you miss him most, "you're a nurturer who takes life very seriously—and relies on witty friends to lighten your load," says McCallum. You also:

- Know how to smooth things over!
- Are loyal to your friends throughout your life.

FAST FACT

COURTNEY COX (MONICA) ORIGINALLY TRIED OUT FOR THE PART OF RACHEL!

Take this fun quiz and find out how well you really get along with animals.

1. **When your next-door neighbor's cat has a litter, she asks if you can help find them homes. You decide to:**
   a. Put up signs around town and at work
   b. Call everyone you think might be interested
   c. Volunteer to take one until you find it a home, then probably end up keeping it!

2. **You think that goldfish are:**
   a. Boring—you can't imagine why anyone would want one
   b. Beautiful to watch
   c. Fascinating creatures you can't get enough of

3. **For two mornings, a squirrel has come tapping at your window. You think he might return. You:**
   a. Tap the window playfully, hoping either to encourage—or discourage—a return visit
   b. Put out some stale crusts of bread
   c. Look for special squirrel food sold only in the pet shop

4. **A friend is coming to spend a summer weekend at your house and asks if she can bring her large dog with her. You say:**
   a. "I'd rather you didn't."
   b. "You may, but I prefer you leave the pooch in the yard during the day."
   c. "Great idea!'

5. **How do you feel when you go for an outing at the zoo?**
   a. Okay. You enjoy looking at all the different animals.

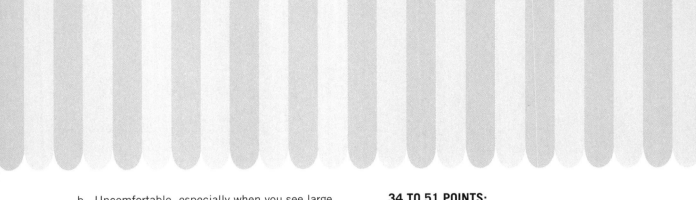

b. Uncomfortable, especially when you see large animals being housed in small cages.

c. Not good. You don't believe wild animals should be taken from their natural habitat.

6. **For Christmas, you give your pet:**
    a. Probably nothing; it wouldn't occur to you to buy a pet a gift
    b. An extra food treat
    c. A new toy

7. **If you owned a parakeet, you'd probably:**
    a. Appreciate its beauty, but that's about it
    b. Try to communicate by imitating it when it chirped
    c. Actively teach it to talk

YOUR SCORE

Give yourself 3 points for each "a" answer,
6 points for every "b," and 9 points for each "c."

21 TO 33 POINTS:
You can appreciate creatures from a distance, but you don't have the patience to spend a lot of time with a pet.

Best bets for you: a pet that requires little attention, such as a fish or a turtle. Try volunteering to care for a friend's pet for a weekend to gain some firsthand experience. The more time you spend with animals, the more comfortable you'll feel around them—and you just might discover you want a pet!

34 TO 51 POINTS:
You're a devoted owner and lavish your pet with all the attention and care needed.

In return, you appreciate the companionship your pet gives to you. But you're not quite as comfortable with other people's animals. You're hesitant to stroke a strange dog or offer your lap to somebody else's cat. The important thing is that you remain responsible to the pet that you own.

52 POINTS OR MORE:
You're practically the Dog Whisperer.

You not only adore animals but you relate to them on a deep level and pick up their subtle cues. Whether it's your own pet, or one passing on the street, you're quick to engage in deep communication. If there's an animal in need, you'll come to its rescue. All kinds of animals win your heart. That's why even the thought of wearing fur makes you miserable!

4. Rate Your Party Panache

Are you the life of the party—or just a pretty wallflower? Take this quiz and see if it's time to add some spark to your style!

1. **You've been asked to be the dinner companion of an important visitor who's known to be difficult and closemouthed. You:**
   a. Politely pass on the honor
   b. Plan to talk a little about yourself, to stimulate conversation
   c. Research his life history and hobbies, so you'll have questions that might loosen him up

2. **You look across a crowded room and find yourself magnetically attracted to a tall, very handsome man. You:**
   a. Forget about it. He's obviously unattainable.
   b. Make eye contact, then look away
   c. Go over and start flirting with him

3. **You've invited a few of your preschooler's friends over. What do you serve for a snack?**
   a. Animal crackers and milk
   b. Cut-up peanut butter or cream cheese and jelly sandwiches
   c. Mini-pizzas and orange "orangutan" juice

4. **How good are you at remembering faces?**
   a. Pretty bad. You have to meet people several times before you get their names straight.
   b. Okay. You have no trouble remembering likable, interesting people.
   c. Great. You've even taught yourself a little trick to remember names.

5. **The dance music is blasting, but you've worn high heels. You:**
   a. Sit it out
   b. Wait for a slow song, then grab a partner
   c. Kick off your shoes and dance barefoot

6. **You've just moved and want to invite new neighbors over for a party. You ask them to:**
   a. Bring a dish for a potluck dinner
   b. Come over between 5:00 and 7:00 p.m. for hors d'oeuvres
   c. Join you for a leisurely brunch

7. **You're on a bus that's stuck in traffic. You:**
   a. Stare out the window
   b. Offer your paper to the person next to you
   c. Start a conversation with those around you, then get almost everyone on the bus involved!

34 TO 51 POINTS:
When it comes to etiquette, you're like Miss Manners.

You always dress just right, whatever the occasion, and treat others with charm and courtesy. But when it comes to enjoying yourself socially, you're a bit too preoccupied. Learn to let go of your worries, at least for a few hours. If you were a little more relaxed you'd really be able have fun. Eat, drink, and be merry. After all, life *is* a party!

52 POINTS OR MORE:
Pop the cork and pour the champagne!

You're a real firecracker at any get-together. You know how to enjoy yourself and help others have fun, too. You're always ready to join in as the major merrymaker. When the conversation is lively and filled with laughter, you're usually the one holding court. Even at the potentially dullest gatherings you can spark things up—and your enthusiasm is catching.

YOUR SCORE

Give yourself 3 points for each "a" answer,
6 points for every "b," and 9 points for each "c."

21 TO 33 POINTS:
You're no party pooper, but you're not the life of the party either.

You feel awkward in large groups, preferring to observe rather than participate. You haven't had much experience as a hostess either. Start by having a dinner for close friends. Once you muster up more courage and master the art of small talk, you'll be able to host a more lavish bash and be a more engaged guest.

5. What Your Friendship Style Reveals about You!

Do you make plans with a friend only if you can't find a date—or would it take a court order to separate the two of you? How you treat your friends—and what you expect from them—says a lot about who you really are. Take this quiz and learn some surprising truths!

1. At a gathering, a very cute guy asks if you'd like to go for a walk. You're supposed to meet a friend in a half hour. You:
   a. Call and cancel. She'll understand.
   b. Ask for a rain check
   c. Bring him along. She won't mind.

2. Your buddy is obviously mulling something over. You say:
   a. Nothing. When she wants to talk, she'll open up.
   b. "Friends share everything. Please tell me what's going on."
   c. "You seem preoccupied. If there's anything I can do to help, let me know—I'll be here for you."

3. You model a skimpy dress for your pal. She suggests you switch to something less revealing. You:
   a. Ignore her. You feel fabulous!
   b. Try to find something a bit more conservative. Her fashion sense is usually impeccable.
   c. Get mad. Who's she to criticize?

4. You met most of your friends in:
   a. The sandbox
   b. High school
   c. The last few years

5. Your dearest friend wins a trip for two to Paris. She invites you, but you can't get time off. She goes with a different friend. You feel:
   a. Like you're being two-timed
   b. Happy for her
   c. Envious—but eagerly anticipate a great souvenir

6. You witness your friend's boyfriend passionately embracing another woman. You:
   a. Phone her immediately—she must know the truth
   b. Forget you ever saw anything
   c. Drop your friend some big hints—or speak directly with her man

7. When a close friend moves to another state, you:
   a. E-mail or call whenever you have something important to tell her
   b. Wait until she contacts you; she's the one who moved
   c. Call her once a week just to see how she's doing

8. You're starting to feel suffocated by an old pal and you need some space. You:
   a. Tell her the truth, although you feel guilty and lousy
   b. Have a heart-to-heart to try to sort things out
   c. Pull away without explanation, canceling plans and avoiding her calls

9. Two of your friends have a vicious fight. You're caught in the middle. You:
   a. Stick with the closer friend and dump the other
   b. Tell them you're neutral
   c. Refuse to speak to either until they make up

10. **Your friend's ex just asked you out. You've always been attracted to him. You:**
    a. Go for it—big time
    b. Tell her. If she doesn't flip out, then it's okay to accept.
    c. Turn him down. It's not worth risking the friendship.

11. **You're working under a tight deadline when your friend calls with something important to say. You:**
    a. Push the papers and problems aside—your ears are all hers
    b. Explain it's a bad time and hang up
    c. Promise to call her back first thing, once your work is done

12. **Your best friend has gotten serious with the jerk of the century. What will you do when she asks if you're happy for her?**
    a. Keep a lid on your concerns
    b. Tell her flat out that he's a badly mannered, dim-witted twit
    c. Casually introduce her to every nice man you know

13. **A friend keeps dropping by without phoning first. You say:**
    a. "Seinfeld's friends drop in anytime; mine phone first!"
    b. Nothing
    c. "It wonderful to see you, but be careful! My doctor says I'm contagious!"

14. **A friend swears you to secrecy, then tells a nasty tidbit of gossip. Later you meet your mate and:**
    a. Tell him not to tell another soul—then spill the beans
    b. Start blabbing before you even kiss him hello
    c. Keep your lips zipped

15. **How do you feel about introducing your friends to each other?**
    a. The more the merrier
    b. You prefer one-on-one, but will get the gang together occasionally
    c. Three's a crowd

YOUR SCORE

Give yourself the following number of points for each answer:

1. a-1, b-3, c-5
2. a-3, b-1, c-5
3. a-3, b-5, c-1
4. a-5, b-3, c-1
5. a-1, b-5, c-3
6. a-5, b-1, c-3
7. a-3, b-1, c-5
8. a-3, b-5, c-1
9. a-1, b-5, c-3
10. a-1, b-3, c-5
11. a-5, b-1, c-3
12. a-3, b-1, c-5
13. a-5, b-3, c-1
14. a-3, b-1, c-5
15. a-3, b-5, c-1

30 POINTS OR LESS:
Can we tell you the truth, girlfriend?

Here it comes: it's a wonder you have any friends! What's the problem? You're either indifferent or occasionally hostile toward them. Maybe you don't understand that your actions and comments can hurt others. Or, as Boston-based psychologist Edith Weinberg sees it: "You may come across as bitchy because you're so lacking in self-confidence that you can't believe your friends would want you involved in their lives in a meaningful way." Good advice: Look for (and celebrate!) reasons to love your pals—and yourself!

31 TO 45 POINTS:
You have difficulty expressing emotions and being sensitive to others' feelings.

"Basically, the inability to communicate is the result of the inability to trust," explains Weinberg. "You probably experienced disappointing relationships either in childhood or later in life. In any case, you clearly have a hard time dealing with intimacy." Make an effort to get closer. Note: If you scored in the high end of this range, there's a possibility you actually prefer distant relationships. If so, no sweat. Tell your friends you need lots of space.

46 TO 60 POINTS:
Your compassion and loyalty have earned you a handful of faithful friends.

Through thick and thin, whenever one of your best pals needs you, you're there. You realize the value of friendship and that's the real reason you would never betray a confidence. You're also honest and tell it like it is. When you give advice, it comes form the heart. "As friend like this is in perfect balance. She feels good about herself and is able to be emotionally generous," says Weinberg. "She's there for friends when they need her, but she's able to sense when it would be better to back off."

61 POINTS OR MORE:
Friends mean everything to you—and there's the snag.

You do anything for them and demand the same loyalty in return. Plus, you tend to be overly concerned with what friends think and feel about you. "Friends should be close," says Weinberg, "but these kind of relationships can be suffocating." Give those around you a little room. And understand that really good friends are able to listen closely and respond as honestly as possible. Let yourself experience occasional twinges of jealousy or anger, even with your closest friends. Finally, be sure your friends are giving as much as you do. "If you're always the one doing more in a relationship," cautions Weinberg, "resentments eventually flare." Aim for a fifty-fifty friendship and go for the gold!

6. These Fragrant Clues Reveal Your Most Cherished Family Memory

The connection between scent and memory is nothing to sniff at: studies of 18,000 people prove the quickest way to bring back the feelings associated with times past is through smell! Why? "Your sense of smell is located in the area of the brain considered the seat of memory and emotions, and the two are connected by a direct pathway—so when one is activated, it triggers the other," explains professional fragrance expert Gail Adrian. "What's more, some of the most evocative scents are those that stem from strong childhood memories, like special holiday times with the family." Pick your favorite autumn aroma—and discover the memories you cherish most!

MAPLE SYRUP:
Your favorite family memories are luxurious!

"Women who are most drawn to the scent of sugary treats value the sense of indulgence they get from life's little luxuries," says Adrian. But your favorite treats aren't just frivolous indulgences! That fluffy duvet you splurged on? It provides soothing slumber! The vacation you saved for? It's a memory your family won't forget! And psychologists say those who have the most happy memories are the most able to make new ones.

SPICED APPLE CIDER:
Your favorite family memories are of achievement!

"Research shows those who are attracted to the invigorating scent of strong spices like nutmeg, cloves, and cinnamon tend to be achievement-oriented extroverts whose most important memories center around early success," says Adrian. A born risk-taker, you're not afraid of being noticed for all that you can do. And when you need an emotional boost, it's the memories to these favorite past achievements that you turn to for your can-do-it inspiration. So whether it's fortune, fame, or just health and happiness, you can use your past to make your future dreams come true!

PINE:
Your favorite family memories are filled with nature!

Studies show that among adults who were born twenty or more years ago, most remember their childhoods being filled with outdoor scents such as grass, animals, and burning leaves! And "pine is one of the sharpest natural scents of all, acting on the brain to bring back memories of running around outdoors with siblings and pals," says Adrian. Your youthful attitude endears you to all the children in your life—and gives you the same exuberant joy you felt when you were a kid!

A ROARING FIRE:
Your favorite memories are of togetherness!

If the scent of a fire is your favorite, odds are you cherish family memories like baking cookies with your mom, spending lazy Sunday mornings reading the comics, and joining in neighborhood block parties and potlucks. Researchers say a fireplace (or hearth) is also a symbol of a warm, generous heart. And, since you know there's nothing more important than a loving family, you keep those home fires roaring merrily.

7. What Do You "Really" Know about Children?

Take this quiz and find out if you're a klutz when it comes to kid care … or ready for a PhD in child development!

1. **If your child is a constant thumb-sucker, the one thing you should not do is:**
   a. Feed your baby whenever he's hungry
   b. Point your finger at his thumb-sucking
   c. Let baby suck only after meal time is over

2. **You've got a tubby toddler. What's the warning sign that she's not pleasingly plump but rather frighteningly fat?**
   a. Her fleshy thighs can't fit into her tights.
   b. Her happy face is as round as a beach ball.
   c. Her belly shakes like a bowl of jelly.

3. **Here's a statement you can sink your teeth into— the first tooth to appear is usually the:**
   a. Molar
   b. Central incisor
   c. Cuspid

4. **These days, Jennifer is a popular name. It's derived from:**
   a. Hebrew, meaning "God is good."
   b. Old French, for "joy."
   c. Welsh, from "Guinevere."

5. **You take your tot out with you for a late dinner. When you finally put her to bed, she'll probably be:**
   a. Delighted. Strange situations are exhausting but fun.
   b. Kick up a fuss. Children need a regular bed time schedule and routine.
   c. Expect a lullaby. Music soothes small night owls.

6. **Not *all* our kids are couch potatoes. How many children participate in their school's extracurricular sports programs?**
   a. 6 million
   b. 20 million
   c. 1 million

7. **Before his first birthday, a baby is most likely to:**
   a. Speak a word you actually understand
   b. Be toilet trained
   c. Pull his wooden duck by a string

8. **Tommy the toddler dreams of a slimy monster and wakes up screaming. To make his nightmare disappear, you should:**
   a. Call the Ghostbusters
   b. Tell him he's being a baby
   c. Hold him tight and try to get him to describe his demon

9. **When Annie smears Silly Putty on her sister's face, it's time to declare a truce. Experts say you can reverse rivalry by conveying:**
   a. Guilt. "I swear you two are giving me an ulcer."
   b. Compassion. "I know you're mad at each other; tell me why."
   c. Anger. "I'm putting the putty away and you two sillies can go to your rooms!"

10. **According to a national survey, what percentage of a teen's diet is snack food?**
    a. 2 percent
    b. 8 percent
    c. 5 percent

YOUR SCORE

The correct answers are:

1. b. Constantly calling attention to a child's thumb-sucking will only make him do it more. Instead, offer other stimuli.

2. a. Toddlers have round faces and tubby tummies, but roly-poly thighs mean fat. If her weight is increasing faster than her height, talk to your doctor about what measures to take.

3. b. Central incisors commonly appear somewhere around the sixth month, next molars, then cuspids.

4. c. Before evolving into today's Jennifer, the name Guinevere enjoyed popularity, as did Winifred.

5. b. Sorry, Mom. Most babies need a steady bed time or they become irregular sleepers.

6. b. Millions of additional kids are enrolled in sports programs outside school, too.

7. c. Lucky ducky!

8. c. Studies show talking about nightmarish monsters makes them less menacing.

9. b. Acknowledging their right to be angry can be a soothing balm for sibling rivals. Good luck!

10. a. See? Your teenager's diet isn't as bad as you thought!

- Give yourself 10 points for each correct answer.

30 POINTS OR LESS:
You're a NON-NANNY.

You don't spend much time around children. Although you think kids are cute, you'd rather observe them from afar. That's a good idea until you work on your patience!

30 TO 79 POINTS:
You're BABY'S BUDDY.

You're not always right when it comes to child development, but you enjoy children and possess common sense when it comes to caring for them.

80 POINTS OR MORE:
You're DR. SPOCK'S RIVAL.

Sensitive and savvy, you have the facts and possess intuitive empathy with little ones. If becoming an authority on kids doesn't ignite your career sparks, perhaps you should consider raising a big family!

8. The True Reason Friends, Family, Neighbors, and Coworkers Love You!

Part One

1. **Your young daughter has had a disagreement with a friend. You:**
   a. Try to distract them by suggesting you all bake cookies together
   b. Let them talk over their feelings

2. **You're meeting your future in-laws for the first time. To make them feel comfortable, you:**
   a. Greet them with a warm, friendly hug
   b. Compliment them on their wonderful son

3. **New folks move in next door. You:**
   a. Invite them to your place to get acquainted
   b. Drop off a casserole. Who wants to cook the first night in a new home?

4. **You have some issues to discuss on parent-teacher conference day. You:**
   a. Begin by telling the teacher how pleased you are with your child's progress
   b. Listen carefully—you'll ask questions later

5. **In a conversation, you:**
   a. Take the lead
   b. Listen attentively

6. **You need a bank loan to market your "Hunk-a-Chunk" cookies. You convince the officer by:**
   a. Exuding confidence
   b. Presenting her with a box of cookies

7. **At gatherings, you can usually be found:**
   a. Meeting new people
   b. Catching up with old friends

8. **A friend is getting over a failed romance, you:**
   a. Introduce her to an interesting single man
   b. Spend time listening to her tale of woe

Part Two

9. **I'm attracted to outgoing people.**
   Agree_____ Disagree_____

10. **People say I'm the life of the party.**
    Agree_____ Disagree_____

11. **My motto is, the more the merrier!**
    Agree_____ Disagree_____

12. **I usually bounce right back from disappointments.**
    Agree_____ Disagree_____

YOUR SCORE

NOTE: If your answers fall equally between the two categories, read both descriptions, since you share characteristics of both types.

MOSTLY A'S AND "AGREE"S:
You're energetic and enthusiastic.

People are always impressed with your unbridled energy and boundless zest for life. You can't help being the life of the party! Your enthusiasm is contagious, and you're able to bring anyone out of their doldrums. Those lucky enough to be in the path of your shining goodwill feel like following your positive lead. You're generous with your time and energy and are always willing to lend a hand, tackle a chore, or join in a special event. Your flame burns bright, warming the hearts of those around you.

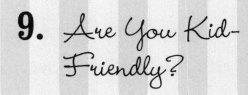

MOSTLY B'S AND "DISAGREE"S:
You're compassionate and empathetic.

You have the ability to put yourself in others' shoes. For this reason, you always know what approach works best. You appreciate the power of listening and make it a point to be attentive. When family and friends have problems, they come to you for advice because they know you're compassionate and slow to judge. Children are especially attracted to your patience and kindness. You're a trustworthy, empathetic person whose open and generous soul is appreciated by many.

FAST FACT

SEVENTY-SIX PERCENT OF US CONSIDER HUMOR TO BE A TOP PERSONALITY TRAIT WHEN CHOOSING FRIENDS!

Do you have a hard time talking to the under-six gang, or are you a Pied Piper with small fry? Take this quiz and discover your gift with kids.

1. **Compared to your friends, your energy level is:**
   a. Wired for fast speed. You can go all day without even taking a break.
   b. Slow and mellow. Everything gets done, but only at your own steady pace.
   c. Flexible. You're quick to act if you must but you prefer to move in the groove.

2. **Which of these joke exchanges tickles your funny bone?** *Knock. Knock. Who's there*?
   a. Orange. Orange who? Orange you glad I didn't say banana?
   b. Banana. Banana who? Banana Head!
   c. Neither. I think all knock-knock jokes are stupid.

3. **When you go to the circus, you think to yourself:**
   a. Poor animals—how they must suffer!
   b. It's amusing but you'd much rather go to the theater
   c. What fun! There's nothing better than to spend a day under the Big Top.

4. **Memories of your own childhood are:**
   a. Great! You recall being pampered.
   b. Not great. Your folks would never win the award for Parents of the Year.
   c. Bittersweet

5. **You're most attracted to colors that are:**
   a. Neutral (browns, beiges, grays)
   b. Bright (zingy reds, hot pinks, pearly blues)
   c. Pale (soft hues of baby blue, powder-puff pink, lime green)

6. **Who's Ernie?**
   a. A comic strip character
   b. A *Sesame Street* regular
   c. A star of a popular sitcom

7. **If a kid asked you to take her for fast food, you would say:**
   a. "Yippee!" and would order a double cheese burger, french fries, and a strawberry malt
   b. "Well, okay," but would try to convince her to reconsider
   c. "Absolutely not." There are empty calories in fast food.

8. **At a family gathering, you spend the most time with your:**
   a. Cousins. You have the most in common.
   b. Grandparents. Their wisdom and unconditional love enrich your life.
   c. Nieces and nephews. Their innocence and antics are endearing.

Part Two

1. **Children are well described as "postcards from home."**
   Agree_____   Disagree_____

2. **I delight in running barefoot through the summer grass and rolling down gentle hills.**
   Agree_____   Disagree_____

3. **If you use sense and take just a bit of care, you cannot spoil a child with too much love.**
   Agree_____   Disagree_____

4. **Basically, I prefer seeing animated fantasy films and lighthearted movies that have happy endings.**
   Agree_____   Disagree_____

5. **I thoroughly enjoy keeping track of all the latest fads.**
   Agree_____   Disagree_____

YOUR SCORE

- For Part One, give yourself the following number of points for each answer.

1. a-5, b-3, c-5	5. a-3, b-7, c-5
2. a-5, b-7, c-3	6. a-5, b-7, c-3
3. a-3, b-5, c-7	7. a-7, b-5, c-3
4. a-7, b-3, c-5	8. a-5, b-3, c-7

- For Part Two, give yourself 3 points for each statement with which you agree.

- Add the scores from Parts One and Two.

39 POINTS OR LESS:
Set in your ways, you find it hard to be around children.

Either your parenting days are past or you're just not ready to spend time with kids. You see your own agenda and like to stick to business—without interruption. Not big on frivolous games or make-believe, you get very little pleasure seeing the world through the eyes of a child. Although you think kids are cute and you're never cruel or un-kind to little ones, you prefer to surround yourself with those old enough to vote. Grown-ups, not those still growing, are your best companions.

40 TO 55 POINTS:

You enjoy spending time with toddlers and young adults as long as it doesn't involve the whole day—every day.

If you have young children, a part-time nanny or day care center is probably your best bet. You need time alone to recharge. Once you're well-rested, your happy-go lucky attitude is a natural magnet for little ones. They love your robust laughter and playful antics. Physically agile, you can keep up with your littlest friend—playing ball, jumping rope, or chasing a Frisbee. In fact, you're often the one to suggest a game of hide-and-seek. When it comes to fun, you're always first in line!

56 POINTS OR MORE:

"Out of the mouths of babes" is your motto.

You honestly feel the greatest lessons can be learned by listening to children. Because they sense your respect, they love to be around you—and vice versa. You can spend all day with children and never miss the company of adults. You think nothing of dressing as a clown, crawling on the floor, or miming a story, as long as it brings smiles to the faces of little ones. If you don't already have a big, bustling family—you should. You know the future is in our children's hearts—and with your help, we have some glorious days ahead!

FAST FACT

WHEN WE GET TOGETHER WITH FRIENDS, 65 PERCENT OF US WOULD RATHER STAY IN THEN GO OUT.

1. **An old pal is distraught because her teenage daughter is planning on joining a rock band and going on the road, instead of going to college. You:**
   a. Calm her down, pointing out that teens are always coming up with wild schemes and they quickly forget
   b. Suggest she and her daughter get together with the school guidance counselor, who could help the girl find a way to follow her heart and get an education

2. **At her wedding shower, your younger sister confides that she has cold feet. You:**
   a. Tell her not to worry. Jitters are normal and they eventually pass.
   b. Ask questions about her concerns, then help her work through her feelings

3. **Your sister-in-law is in tears over her new (not-so-flattering) haircut. You make her feel better by saying:**
   a. "It's really not that bad. Besides, it will grow out in no time!"
   b. "Call the salon. I'm sure they'd be willing to fix it for free."

4. **A coworker asks you to help her prepare for a job interview. Your tactic:**
   a. Psyching her up by listing all her on-the-job strengths
   b. Staging a mock interview and offering answers to questions she might stumble over

5. **You're not very impressed with the girl your son just met. When he asks your opinion, you tell him:**
   a. You're sure she's a lovely person once you really get to know her
   b. A few things about her that make you uneasy

6. **You're in your friend's kitchen while she nervously prepares a dish for dinner guests. You:**
   a. Tell her that everything looks delicious
   b. Taste the dish and let her know if any need a little of this or that

7. **When a coworker starts taking a "miracle" diet pill, you:**
   a. Wish her well. You know from experience that positive reinforcement really helps when you're losing weight.
   b. Urge her to call her doctor. If the pill is bogus, he could recommend something that might really work.

YOUR SCORE

NOTE: If your answers fall equally between the two categories, read both descriptions since you share characteristics of both types.

MOSTLY A'S:
You're soothing.

Nonjudgmental and reassuring, you're the type of person others eagerly seek out for advice—especially when they're feeling vulnerable. You prefer to bring out the positive side of situations rather than dwell on doubts, and that approach is a sure mood lifter. Your way of giving advice also provides comfort and instills confidence, which is often enough to turn negative situations around!

MOSTLY B'S:
You're a problem solver.

Blessed with keen insight and a no-nonsense personality, you truly enjoy the challenge of resolving problems presented to you—no matter how big or how small they may be. Others have come to expect genuine help from you—and you always deliver! That's why your reputation for being so honest and wise is well deserved!

FAST FACT

SURVEYS SHOW THAT MOST OF PREFER TO HEAR BAD NEWS BEFORE GOOD NEWS.

11. How Do You Communicate with Friends?
The answer is right on your lips!

New studies show a powerful connection between your favorite lipstick shade and the way you communicate with others. "Color sends a strong signal about how we see ourselves—and how we want to be seen," says Leatrice Eiseman, author of *Colors for Your Every Mood.* See what your lipstick is saying about you.

IF YOUR LIPSTICK IS BRIGHT RED:
Your communication style is high energy!

"Women who love this shade are energetic and driven!" says Eiseman. It's no surprise that:

- You make sure you know a little something about everything and everyone.
- You leap into love and life with fiery enthusiasm—because research proves red causes a hormonal surge that makes you passionate!

IF YOUR LIPSTICK IS CLEAR:
Your communication style is tell-it-like-it-is talker!

Gloss-wearers are no-nonsense types who like to keep it simple—"which means speaking your mind without embellishing the facts," says Eiseman. And that's why:

- Your balanced view makes it easy for you to stay neutral in sticky situations.
- Your wardrobe is full of classic staples.
- Studies show direct types like you keep conversations short and sweet—getting right to the heart of the matter!

IF YOUR LIPSTICK IS ORANGE:
Your communication style is happy-go-lucky chatterbox.

To the ancient Chinese, orange symbolized joy, so it's no wonder "orange lipstick wearers are fun-loving social butterflies!" says Eiseman. And:

- Your perfect evening is spent catching up with family and friends.
- Research shows folks who love to talk are also great multitaskers!

IF YOUR LIPSTICK IS PINK:
Your communication style is soft-spoken.

"Women who like pink tend to be soft-spoken types who make their point gently," says Eiseman. What else?

- Studies show your soft touch puts people at ease.
- You're a natural stress buster, since research shows people who like pink have lower blood pressure, pulse, and heart rates!

IF YOUR LIPSTICK IS DARK RED OR BROWN:
Your communication style is friendly conversationalist.

These are the colors of the earth, and "women who choose them project that same dependability and nurturing influence," says Eiseman. Which means:

- You rate high on scales of honesty!
- You express yourself simply, using down-to-earth language.
- You bring a welcoming touch to your decor, creating a cozy nest that's perfect for intimate conversation!

FAST FACT

THIRTY-SEVEN PERCENT OF MEN SAY THEY LIKE BARE LIPS BEST—BUT WHEN IT COMES TO COLOR, RUBY RED AND HOT PINK TOP THEIR LIST!

Of course, every woman's biggest and most important role model is her mom—and that's great! But a brand-new survey shows that the famous woman you admire most says a lot about how you reach your goals! "That's because we almost always identify with the well-known person who shares the very same values and priorities that we cherish," says historian Catherine Allgor, PhD, professor at the University of California at Riverside. These are the four women most often chosen in surveys as America's top role models—choose the one you admire most, and discover the hidden reason you deserve recognition!

OPRAH WINFREY:
You're a great talker and listener!

When it comes to getting her message across, no one surpasses Oprah! "An excellent communicator, she's all about connecting with others in a positive, uplifting, and inspiring way," says Allgor. If you admire her, chances are you're also extremely tuned into the feelings, needs, and perspectives of those around you. A friend seems down? You chat with her until she reveals what's wrong—and then help her make it right! Intuitive enough to tap into the feelings of loved ones and sensitive enough to know just what to say, you talk your way to happiness and prosperity.

HILLARY RODHAM CLINTON:
You're a superachiever.

Bright and motivated, Hillary put her own high ambitions on hold while she stood by her husband—and then went full steam ahead! If Hillary's your role model, you're also a driven overachiever who never backs away from a challenge," says Allgor. Whether it's starting your own business, running for local government, or just socking away money for your dream vacations, you strive until you achieve your goal. Your persistence means that you've got success to spare!

JULIA ROBERTS:
You radiate optimism.

"Of course, Julia Roberts is gorgeous and famous—but it's her upbeat attitude that draws the most admirers," says Allgor. Her positive outlook and friendly demeanor shows in everything she does—and if you relate to her, so do yours! With an optimism that gets you through any rough spot, you're able to shake off disappointment and find the bright side in any situation. You may not live in Hollywood, but you're a real shining star!

LAURA BUSH:
You're strong and centered.

If your life is like a tornado, then you're the eye of the storm! Just like you, Laura Bush is the calming force in the wind of divisive politics. "She projects a sense of serenity and friendly well-being no matter what the occasion," says Allgor. So do you: even when your family needs breakfast, the phone's ringing off the hook, and the washing machine has just overflowed, you stay steady, offering solutions and a helping hand. Your family looks to you to pull them through—because you're the poster girl for grace under pressure.

13. Are Your Friends and Family Giving You Enough Attention?

1. **There's nothing in the cupboard for dinner. What's your family likely to do?**
   a. Go out to a restaurant of your choice.
   b. Order in—your husband will pick it up on his way home.
   c. Wait for you to get back from the grocery store with the fixings.

2. **Congratulations! You just won a shopping spree at a department store! Where do you head first?**
   a. Designer dresses—yippee!
   b. Cosmetics—you'd love some tips!
   c. Handbags—yours are worn out.

3. **In the past, when your birthday's landed on a workday:**
   a. Your colleagues bought a cake, chipped in for a gift, and signed a card
   b. Your closest coworker treated you to lunch
   c. You received a bunch of cards, good wishes, and smiles

4. **At the end of the day, you usually feel:**
   a. Glad about everything you've accomplished
   b. Tired sometimes, but often pretty satisfied
   c. Pooped!

5. **When was the last time you were served breakfast in bed?**
   a. A few weeks ago
   b. Your last birthday
   c. Last fall when you had the flu

6. **Do you feel that whatever you do, you'll always have someone to fall back or rely on?**
   a. Absolutely!
   b. Only up to a point; you'd never want to take advantage of others.
   c. Sure—yourself!

7. **After a long, hard day, you usually:**
   a. Soak in a warm tub
   b. Kvetch to your spouse or friend about the day's trials and tribulations
   c. Pull yourself together to take care of household chores

YOUR SCORE

NOTE: If your answers fall equally between two of the three categories, read more than one description, since you share characteristics of those types.

MOSTLY A'S:
You're positively pampered.

Lucky lady! Your friends, coworkers, and loved ones are generous with their appreciation. But there's no secret to your pampered lifestyle—people are simply returning all the wonderful attention you pay to them!

MOSTLY B'S:
You're just shy of satisfied.

Although you're basically happy, you do have moments when you crave more attention. But have you ever thought to ask? Remember that to gain some time in the limelight, you may have to push your way onstage—let others know exactly what you need and you'll get it!

MOSTLY C'S:

You're an unsung heroine.

There are times when your good deeds or tireless efforts go unnoticed … and naturally, you feel disappointed. Speak up; if reminding others of your worth doesn't get results, try taking a hiatus from some of your selfless habits—see how quickly friends, family members, and coworkers show their gratitude.

FAST FACT

FORTY-THREE PERCENT OF WIVES THINK THEIR HUSBANDS GET MORE TIME TO THEMSELVES THAN THEY DO.

---

14. Are You a Meddler?

Do you find it impossible to keep your nose out of other people's business? Take this quiz and see if you're interfering too much!

Part One

1. **The man in line ahead of you hasn't budged. You:**
   a. Tell him to go!
   b. Wait patiently
   c. Bellow "Next!"

2. **Your friend is putting on weight, so you:**
   a. Ask if she wants your fat Aunt Fanny's old clothes
   b. Say nothing
   c. Give her diet treats

3. **You bump into your sister's husband—with another woman! You:**
   a. Phone Sis pronto!
   b. Pull him aside and insist on the real scoop
   c. Stay out of it

4. **Your neighbor shows you her bedroom—which looks like a bordello. You:**
   a. Blush!
   b. Buy her a red satin bedspread
   c. Ask if she wanted it to look so sleazy

5. **The class bully has been picking on your son. You:**
   a. Tell the bully to bug off
   b. Speak to the teacher
   c. Teach your son to turn the other cheek

6. **If your spouse was feeling blue, you would:**
   a. Distract him with a new look
   b. Tell him to snap out of it
   c. Act sunnier than usual

7. **When you see a stranger drop a candy wrapper on the street, you:**
   a. Look the other way
   b. Shout "Litter bug!"
   c. Pick it up and throw it in the trash

8. **Your favorite TV show is canceled. You:**
   a. Change channels
   b. Call the station
   c. Start a petition

Part Two

1. **I'm active in community projects.**
   Agree_____ Disagree_____

2. **Just call me Ms. Lonely Hearts.**
   Agree_____ Disagree_____

3. **When a coworker isn't pulling her weight, I feel it's my responsibility to tell the boss.**
   Agree_____ Disagree_____

4. **There are so many issues I'm concerned about, I'm always writing letters to the editor of our local newspaper.**
   Agree_____ Disagree_____

5. **Whenever I visit someone, I love to offer my decorating expertise.**
   Agree_____ Disagree_____

YOUR SCORE

For Part One, give yourself the following number of points for each answer:

1. a-5, b-3, c-7
2. a-7, b-5, c-3
3. a-7, b-5, c-3
4. a-3, b-5, c-7
5. a-7, b-5, c-3
6. a-5, b-7, b-3
7. a-3, b-7, c-5
8. a-3, b-5, c-7

- For Part Two, give yourself 3 points for each statement with which you agree.

- Add the scores from Parts One and Two.

39 POINTS OR LESS:
Basically, you believe in privacy— both your own and others'.

Your philosophy is simple: what goes on behind closed doors is nobody's business. But you sometimes take your personal philosophy too far. When friends, lovers, or relatives seek advice or want to discuss their personal lives, try not to tune out or change the subject. At first, you may feel awkward since you grew up in a home where personal problems were never discussed. But the only way to establish a close relationship is to open the channels of communication. Remember, sharing is not snooping.

40 TO 55 POINTS:
You have a keen interest in human nature, the ability to feel compassion, and a knack for offering helpful advice.

These combined traits help you enjoy learning about other people's lives. Nothing makes you happier than to hear a tasty bit of gossip. Although this may appear to be meddling, it's more a matter of exploration. Since you never try to interfere in anyone's else's business, you really aren't a meddler. However, it would be better if you turned your interest in a more productive direction. Perhaps you should consider a career as a therapist or counselor?

56 POINTS OR MORE:
You can no more mind your business than eat air for survival.

A self-appointed busybody, you poke around personal lives as a prospector would search for gold. But consider this: it's more important to "know thyself" than to put your two cents into everybody else's private affairs. You're smart, curious, and ingenious, and all these qualities can help you discover your own truths. Become the master of your own life instead of meddling in others' lives.

15. Have You Been Typecast?

We all have a role we play with our family, a special strength they count on, says stress expert Debbie Mandel, author of *Turn On Your Inner Light*. How have you been typecast? Find out!

1. **When you feel the sniffles coming on, to chase them away you:**
   a. Take a cold remedy
   b. Ignore it and go on as usual
   c. Get to bed early
   d. Make a soothing pot of tea

2. **The last time you had some extra cash, you:**
   a. Bought yourself a fabulous outfit or piece of jewelry
   b. Bought a new TV, computer, or other gadget
   c. Booked a getaway with someone special
   d. Surprised a loved one with a special gift

3. **When a friend is having a tough time, you:**
   a. Suggest lots of solutions for her to try
   b. Do everything in your power to help her
   c. Try to distract her
   d. Let her know you're there to listen

4. **How do you react to an unexpected gift?**
   a. With immediate thoughts about what you should give in return
   b. With a twinge of embarrassment
   c. With heartfelt pleasure
   d. With a big hug

5. **At a party, you're more likely to chat about:**
   a. What's in the headlines
   b. Your job
   c. A spiritual issue
   d. The latest accomplishments of your family

6. **What are you most likely to do when you have a free evening at home?**
   a. Chat on the phone
   b. Catch up on chores
   c. Watch a movie
   d. Bake or cook something special

7. **When you get lost in the car, the first thing you do is:**
   a. Get out the map
   b. Retrace your route
   c. Stop at a gas station
   d. Call home or your destination

YOUR SCORE

NOTE: If your answers fall equally between the two categories, read both descriptions, since you share characteristics of both types.

MOSTLY A'S:
You're seen as the PROBLEM SOLVER!

"Your mind whizzes through the pros and cons of every situation—which is why loved ones lean on you to solve their problems, too," says Mandel. To get them to see there's more to you than just troubleshooting:

- Just listen. Studies show seven out of ten times, people just want to vent—which helps them solve their own crisis!
- Show your softer side. Letting others see you have dilemmas—and struggle to find solutions—will make you more "real."

MOSTLY B'S: YOU'RE SEEN AS THE RESPONSIBLE DOER!

The reward for your hard work? Usually more work! That's because you're so reliable that everyone assumes you can handle more and more and more. To break that mold, experts advise you to:

- Delegate. It gives others a chance to share the load—and takes the weight off your shoulders!
- Stand tall! "If you don't look like you carry the weight of the world on your shoulders—by slouching, for example—you won't be expected to," says Mandel.

MOSTLY C'S: YOU'RE SEEN AS THE WORLD'S BEST PAL!

Generous and sentimental, you'd drop everything to help a friend or loved one. "Women who open their hearts as wide as you do empathize so well that they can sometimes 'catch the blues,'" says Mandel. Restore some balance to your life by:

- Enjoying a hobby. Finding something that excites you not only makes you more multidimensional to others, but also more important to yourself.
- Giving yourself a hug—literally. Hugs increase the feel-good hormone serotonin.

MOSTLY D'S: You're seen as the NURTURER!

You make sure every detail of your family's daily life flows smoothly. "But you're such a nurturer that you hardly notice your needs falling by the wayside, until you feel taken for granted," says Mandel. To instill a new sense of appreciation in your loved ones:

- Hand out calendars. That'll teach your family to manage their own time and give you time for yourself.
- Go on strike—just a little bit! "It's good for your family to pitch in around the house—it teaches them just how much you do!" says Mandel.

16. Take the Ultimate Test of Class—

Are You the Queen of Tact or Princess Graceless?

True class has nothing to do with social rank. You can be the queen of the planet and possess not an iota of good taste. But if you can sail over difficult situations with cool reserve, offer charm and sophistication to strangers, employ the proper etiquette, and temper tacky embarrassments with polish and grace, then you go to the head of the class. Take the ultimate test and see where you stand.

1. **Your man insists on telling you about love affairs. You react by:**
   a. Wanting to know every detail of his past experiences
   b. Feeling rather jealous and resentful
   c. Telling him you're not comfortable hearing about his past love life
   d. Sharing the steamiest details of your romance stories

2. **A group you're with begins to criticize a friend of yours in rather harsh terms. What's more, most of what they're saying is untrue. You:**
   a. Walk away from the conversation so you won't be asked to join in
   b. Defend her fiercely
   c. Make it clear she's your friend and that their comments are unjustified
   d. Listen carefully to what they're saying so you can report back to her

3. **You are served a plate of asparagus. You eat it:**
   a. With your fingers
   b. Not at all. You despise those slimy green stalks.
   c. With a knife and fork
   d. Daintily, with an appetizer fork

4. **You're planning a trip abroad but can't speak the language of the country you're visiting. You:**
   a. Resort to sign language
   b. Speak in clear, concise English
   c. Don't go. You'd rather not face the embarrassment.
   d. Take along a foreign-language phrase book

5. **While dining out, you get into a heated argument with your partner about an issue that's important to you. You:**
   a. Leave the restaurant
   b. Pretend to outsiders that all is well until you can work it out
   c. Keep sparring until he admits he's wrong
   d. Fall silent

6. **You're cornered at a party by an always-on-call insurance salesman. You:**
   a. Excuse yourself for a visit to the powder room

b. Keep smiling, hoping he'll soon move on to someone else

c. Tell him you simply aren't interested in what he has to say

d. Politely make an excuse, then move across the room to talk to someone else

7. **Your boss is telling you about his new advertising program, which, frankly, you think is a bad idea. You:**

   a. Compliment his plan, hoping to get points for massaging his ego

   b. Refrain from saying anything either way

   c. Praise it for whatever minor points you think have promise while mentioning some of your objections

   d. Tell him bluntly why you think it won't work and hope he'll see the light

YOUR SCORE

Give yourself the following number of points for each answer:

1. a-7, b-5, c-10, d-3   5. a-3, b-10, c-5, d-7
2. a-5, b-7, c-10, d-3   6. a-10, b-7, c-3, d-5
3. a-10, b-3, c-7, d-5   7. a-5, b-7, c-10, d-3
4. a-7, b-5, c-3, d-10

60 TO 70 POINTS:
You possess a natural charm and civility that makes you stand out in the elegance department.

No matter what the situation, you wear your kid gloves and handle any crisis with sophistication and refinement. Somehow, you manage to know intuitively the manner with which to present yourself. You embody pure grace and sophistication; your breeding is classic.

40 TO 50 POINTS:
Raised by your parents to consider the feelings of others,

you usually present yourself in social situations with polish and tact. Your manners are always impeccable. But occasionally you let off steam rather than surveying the situation with calm and reserve. When matters affect you personally, that's the time to pay attention to your tact.

20 TO 30 POINTS:
Princess Graceless, you're a bit too crass and indelicate.

You blurt out your emotions without screening them propriety. Remember, you catch more flies with honey than vinegar. So sweeten up with a bit of charm.

FEWER THAN 20 POINTS:
When it comes to your standing in class, you should be left back.

Register for a crash course in refinement.

17. The Friendship Secrets in Your Favorite Pizza
Find Out What Your Buddies Admire Most in You!

Studies show that human flavor preferences are usually set by age seven—the same time our permanent personality traits develop. But inexplicably, researchers have found there's one flavor preference that's an exception: pizza topping! Everyone loves the crunchy crust and melting cheese, "But your favorite topping is a choice that grows and changes over your lifetime, because what you like depends on who you are at any particular point in time," says researcher Ed Treacy of Domino's Pizza. So grab a slice of your current favorite—and discover a slice of your life!

A NEW CLASSIC, SUCH AS "MARGHERITA":
You're a chameleon!

Those who prefer newer pizzas (like barbecue chicken or margherita with basil) are always open to change. Flexible and creative, you consider new experiences key to your happiness!

THE WORKS!
You're an outgoing adventurer.

"Pizza eaters who pile on the toppings are outgoing risk takers who have a natural zest for adventure!" reveals Treacy. You're always open to possibility—which makes every day a smorgasbord of tasty offerings.

PLAIN CHEESE:
You're a down-to-earth doer!

Hey, Miss Practicality! No drama-queen attitude for you—you think of yourself as calm, capable, and can-do, and you prove it by handling any task with relaxed, no-nonsense panache. No wonder plain pizza is the most overwhelming favorite of stay-at-home moms!

AN EXOTIC COMBINATION:
You see yourself as a real original.

Whether you like your pie topped with pineapple and ham, artichokes and bacon, or anchovies and olives, you're a one-of-a-kind original. You do away with convention—and go after what makes you happy instead!

PEPPERONI:
You're a people pleaser!

Join the crowd, because you just picked America's number one topping! "Pepperoni is the choice of folks who like to be in the center of the action; they're happy to go along with the crowd, possess a strong sense of community, and enjoy being in the mainstream," says Treacy.

FAST FACT

FOR REASONS THAT BAFFLE EXPERTS, FOLKS WHO HANG WIND CHIMES ON THE FRONT PORCH ARE FOUR TIMES MORE LIKELY TO ORDER OLIVES ON THEIR PIZZA!

18. How Do You Relate to Others?

The Answer Is in a Box of Chocolates!

Picture yourself sitting down with a big, heart-shaped box of chocolates. Which of the delicious morsels do you reach for first? Your choice reveals more than you think! "Studies of more than 18,000 people show that chocolate evokes some of the most treasured and important memories of our childhood—a time when we felt freest and most confident to just be ourselves and show off our true personality traits," explains candy expert Susan Fussell of the Chocolate Manufacturers Association. That's why even today your favorite chocolate reveals secrets about the way you connect with others.

TRUFFLES:
You expect the best!

More than any other type of chocolate, there's an opulent, indulgent quality to the truffle. "Surveys show that folks who choose it have a strong appreciation for the finer things," says Fussell. And just like them, you see yourself as worthy of the best—and that includes friendships, romantic partners, and material goods. Even if you can't afford the finest silk blouse, you know that treating yourself to the nicest things you can afford is one of the best ways to celebrate your own extra-special flair! And you're always the first one to reach for the check and treat others!

CHERRY CENTER:
You're a bit of a loner.

There it sits all by itself: the foil-wrapped chocolate-covered cherry, the only one in the box. "Marketing surveys show that folks who reach for this unusual chocolate first have the confidence to stand alone and be a touch different—and they pride themselves on their independence," reveals Fussell. Never one to run with the crowd, you feel unique inside, and you want others to know it! Everyone else is bundled up in a parka? You don a glamorous vintage overcoat! The whole neighborhood heads to the movies for the latest

blockbuster? You stroll to the art house for an independent film! You enjoy feeling creative and offbeat—always an original in a sea of sameness.

SOLID CHOCOLATE WITH NUTS:
You're dependable as a rock.

"Our studies show that people who prefer hard chocolate with nuts frequently score high on scales of good old-fashioned backbone," says Fussell. You see yourself as the rock in your family and you pride yourself on your ability to create a secure environment for them. Seeing to the little things makes you feel as if you're building a strong foundation on which you and your loved ones can stand, grow—and reach for the stars!

CREAM CENTER:
You're steadfast and loyal.

There are more cream-filled chocolates in most assortments than any other kind—because surveys by the Chocolate Manufacturers Association show they're the most popular! "These are the tried and true standbys—and industry research shows folks who like them best are solid traditionalists who prefer the known quantity rather than experiment," says Fussell—and that goes for products, people, and even your career! Slightly suspicious of anything slick and new, you view yourself as a protector of the way things used to be, whether it's your parents' solid values, your community's cohesiveness, or your country's sense of pride. You're steadfast and loyal—and you want it to show!

CARAMEL CENTER:
You're a kid at heart!

If you love to hunt for the chocolate-covered caramels, you've never lost your love for good old-fashioned fun. "Caramels hold a hallowed place in the world of chocolate: they're an uncomplicated standard that everyone learns to love when they're young," says Fussell. No wonder they're the number one favorite among kids! If you still love them, you're fun-loving, enthusiastic, and young at heart! It's no wonder friends and family want to hang out with you. They know there's a guaranteed blast to be had!

FAST FACT:

IN THE 1800S, DOCTORS REGULARLY ADVISED LOVELORN PATIENTS TO EAT PLENTY OF CHOCOLATE—BECAUSE THEY BELIEVED IT WOULD MAKE THEM FALL OUT OF LOVE!

19. Are You Good Mommy Material?

Does the thought of holding a tiny baby in your arms fill you with joy—or panic? Take this quiz and see if it's time to fill your nursery!

Part One

1. **If you had to choose one thing you couldn't give up, it would be:**
   a. Sleep. Without eight hours, you're short-tempered.
   b. Free time. You love to pamper yourself.
   c. Exercise

2. **Your two-year-old doesn't want to finish her farina. You would:**
   a. Ask if she wants more. If not, clear the table.
   b. Threaten to take away her favorite toy
   c. Tell her no sweet snack later unless she cleans her plate

3. **Which fairy tale best describes your childhood?**
   a. *Hansel and Gretel*—your parents were always trying to get rid of you.
   b. *Peter Pan*—Your life was a great adventure!
   c. *The Ugly Duckling*—Need you say more?

4. **You love to spend vacation time:**
   a. In the woods
   b. In a five-star hotel room with your honey
   c. With family

5. **How important is your career?**
   a. It's your number-one priority right now.
   b. What career?
   c. It matters, but not more than motherhood.

6. **We won't tell—how old are you?**
   a. Under 25
   b. Between 25 and 39
   c. Over 39

7. **Your six-year-old is cursing. You would:**
   a. Find out where he's learning his language
   b. Ignore him
   c. Say a few choice words to him!

8. **If you had to choose a name for your baby from this list, you'd pick:**
   a. Anastasia Marie
   b. China Sunshine
   c. Jennifer Grace

Part Two

1. **There's no such thing as spoiling a newborn.**
   Agree_____   Disagree_____

2. **One thing a child can't do without is love.**
   Agree_____   Disagree_____

3. **I'm very close to my mother.**
   Agree_____   Disagree_____

4. **Frankly, I'm not a perfectionist.**
   Agree_____   Disagree_____

5. **Parents should share equal responsibility for raising their kids.**
   Agree_____   Disagree_____

YOUR SCORE

For Part One, give yourself the following number of points for each answer:

1. a-3, b-5, c-7
2. a-7, b-3, c-5
3. a-3, b-7, c-5
4. a-5, b-3, c-7
5. a-3, b-7, c-5
6. a-3, b-7, c-5
7. a-7, b-5, c-3
8. a-5, b-3, c-7

- For Part Two, give yourself 3 points for each statement with which you agree.

- Add the scores from Parts One and Two.

39 POINTS OR LESS:
Wrapped up in a world you worked very hard to create, you have no space for motherhood.

For now, your career takes top priority. Clear signals you're not on the Mommy Track: an inability to survive on less than nine hours of sleep and a horrified feeling at the sight of fingerprinted doors. However, you could make a lovely aunt. Every child needs not only a mother, but a mentor, too. Share your special gifts with a little one and you'll both reap rich rewards.

40 TO 55 POINTS:
Basically, you have what it takes to be a terrific mother.

You're patient, imaginative, responsible, and loving. We would say you'd make a wonderful mother if only your romantic life were together. You expend a tremendous amount of energy trying to smooth over the rocky road your relationship travels. Young children need tons of love and attention, and they'll only suffer if you're distracted by your own problems. Learn to live happily with the man in your life, or make a change. Once you do, you'll be grade-A mommy material.

56 POINTS OR MORE:
The call, "Mommy, Mommy, Mommy" is music to your ears.

Although other women might prefer to cruise on a leisure yacht or share a romantic candlelit dinner, you crave the warm pleasures of an evening at home with the family. Since your own childhood was almost idyllic, you know what makes kids happiest. You're steady, easygoing, generous, and, most important, loving in a nonjudgmental way. If you're already a mother, you know how right it feels. If not, choose a career that keeps you in contact with kids. You've got what it takes—and more!

20. *How Much Do You Trust People?*

Part One

1. **You need a new microwave oven and an ad in the newspaper says "Microwave Sale! Rock Bottom Prices!" You:**
   a. Race to the store before they sell out
   b. Comparison-shop before you go

2. **It looks cloudy, but the weather report promised sunshine. You:**
   a. Dress for sunny weather
   b. Bring an umbrella

3. **You try on a dress and the saleswoman says you look fabulous. You:**
   a. Buy it. After all, she's an expert.
   b. Bring a friend with you to get another opinion

4. **When you withdraw money from the cash machine, do you always count it?**
   a. No. I've never had a problem.
   b. Yes. Even machines can be wrong.

5. **You are more likely to give to a charity that:**
   a. Sends a letter that tugs on your heartstrings
   b. Is well known, such as the American Red Cross

6. **You hire a plumber based on:**
   a. His ad in the paper
   b. His references

7. **If you bought an appliance that came with a warranty, you would probably:**
   a. Throw the warranty form away
   b. Mail the warranty in immediately

8. **Your hairdresser says, "I want to give you a new look."**
   a. You tell her to go ahead—she's known you for a long time.
   b. You insist she show you a photograph of the style

Part Two

9. **I don't pay too much attention to fine print.**
   Agree_____   Disagree_____

10. **I make most decisions based on my intuition.**
    Agree_____   Disagree_____

11. **When my teenager explains why he missed his curfew, I believe him.**
    Agree_____   Disagree_____

12. **I often buy products based on advertising claims.**
    Agree_____   Disagree_____

13. **People have told me that I'm gullible.**
    Agree_____   Disagree_____

YOUR SCORE

NOTE: If your answers fall equally between the two categories, read both descriptions, since you share characteristics of both types.

MOSTLY A'S AND "AGREE"S:
You are totally trusting.

There is no room for doubt or distrust in your life. Instead, you have faith people will do the right thing and, thankfully, you are rarely proven wrong. Others react to your trusting nature positively and try to live up to your expectations. Your faith that there is basic goodness in the world gives you an optimistic and sunny outlook on life. You are able to forge ahead without letting disappointments hold you back. You maintain wonderful relationships with friends and coworkers because you are so open and trusting.

MOSTLY B'S AND "DISAGREE"S:
You are a little leery.

You possess a healthy amount of skepticism. As a result, you're nobody's fool. You make it a point to read documents carefully before signing, investigate advertising claims before buying, and ask for proof when you are in doubt. You are a person who gives more weight to scientific fact than to intuitive reasoning. When friends and coworkers want to know the facts, they come to you. They know there's no way anybody can pull the wool over your eyes.

"If you want to convince others to see things your way, you have to tap into your personality strengths," says Dave Lakhani, author of *Persuasion: The Art of Getting What You Want.* **Take this test to uncover the skill that will help you turn anyone to your point of view!**

1. **You'd most likely sign a formal letter:**
    a. Sincerely
    b. Regards
    c. All the best

2. **To get a teenager to clean her room, you'd:**
    a. Discuss the house rules—and the consequences for not cleaning up
    b. Promise a reward or gift
    c. Offer to help

3. **To convince an interviewer you're right for a job, you'd stress your:**
    a. Experience and accomplishments
    b. Positive attitude
    c. Willingness to learn and grow

4. **To get your husband to try a new restaurant rather than your family's old standby, you'd:**
    a. Show him some rave reviews from a local paper or guidebook
    b. Double date with a couple you both like
    c. Agree to go to his choice next time

5. **To raise money for a worthy cause, you'd prefer to:**
    a. Write an appeal letter
    b. Organize a talent show
    c. Sell raffle tickets

6. **Of these, you'd probably make a better:**
   a. Lawyer
   b. Motivational speaker
   c. Teacher

YOUR SCORE

NOTE: If your answers fall equally between the two categories, read both descriptions, since you share characteristics of both types.

MOSTLY A'S:
Your persuasive talent is SOUND REASONING.

Governed by logical thinking, you persuade others to see your point of view by using your ability to bring issues into clear focus. Thanks to your intelligence, you can provide specific details that win opponents to your side. "By presenting information precisely, people are comforted—they trust the facts—and are likely to follow your lead," says Lakhani.

MOSTLY B'S:
Your persuasive talent is HUMOR AND WIT.

With an ability to put people at ease and make them laugh, you possess one of the quintessential powers of persuasion. "Studies confirm an optimistic outlook and the ability to look at issues with humor is infectious," says Lakhani. "It draws people to you." This ability to create instant rapport increases your confidence and adds to successful persuasion.

MOSTLY C'S:
Your persuasive talent is FLEXIBITY.

Your willingness to listen carefully and explore all possibilities with a gentle touch leads even the most resistant to your side. Along with your powers of reasoning, you're willing to compromise if you feel your opponent is standing on solid ground. More often than not, though, your flexibility leads others to similarly open their minds—and to share points of view!

22. What Makes You So Utterly Appealing to Close Pals?

"We all have that one special trait that everyone loves about us," says Molly Barrow, PhD, author of *Matchlines*. Take this quiz and discover your most endearing quality—the one that wins everyone's heart!

1. **The type of Valentine's Day card you like to send is:**
   a. Humorous
   b. Simple with a powerful message
   c. Classic and sentimental

2. **If you could be in the audience of one of these shows, you'd choose:**
   a. *The Tonight Show with Jay Leno*
   b. *Deal or No Deal*
   c. *The View*

3. **Of these, the party game you'd most enjoy playing is:**
   a. Pictionary
   b. Truth or Dare
   c. Charades

4. **You find your mate most attractive when he:**
   a. Makes you laugh
   b. Surprises you
   c. Expresses affection

5. **Of these, the exercise that most appeals to you is:**
   a. Dancing or aerobics
   b. Hiking, biking—anything outdoors
   c. Pilates, yoga, or tai chi

6. **The one attraction you won't miss at an amusement park is:**
   a. The haunted house
   b. A roller coaster
   c. The carousel

7. **On a day when everything seems to go wrong, you'd most likely:**
   a. Rent a favorite video to end your day on a happy note
   b. Treat yourself to an impulse purchase
   c. Indulge in your favorite dinner

YOUR SCORE

NOTE: If your answers fall equally between the two categories, read both descriptions, since you share characteristics of both types.

MOSTLY A'S:
Your most lovable quality is your SENSE OF HUMOR!

There's never a dull moment when you're around—and if there is, well, you know just what to say or do to fill it with laughter. Witty and good-natured, you never let life's daily hassles or awkward moments get to you; instead, you combat them with a smile or a humorous take on things that eases even the most uncomfortable situation.

MOSTLY B'S:
Your most lovable quality is your FREE SPIRIT!

Your boundless energy is contagious, and your willingness to explore the unknown inspires others to push themselves to venture into new horizons, too. You never worry about what anyone else thinks of you; you just march to your own drummer. It's that enthusiasm and your sky's-the-limit attitude that make you a standout in any crowd!

MOSTLY C'S:
Your most lovable quality your BIG HEART!

You have the uncanny ability to put yourself in others' shoes and can sense when those you love need some extra TLC. Generous and giving, you not only know how to make everyone feel important, you usually go above and beyond to do it! You're always prepared to do whatever it takes to help out—even at the last minute!

23. What's the Special Gift You Give Your Friends?

Most of us put plenty of thought into the gifts we give. So it's no surprise that you're actually giving away a little something about ourselves in every one of those packages! "The gifts we give to friends says a lot about the way we view those friendships," says New York psychologist Miriam Biddleman. You prefer to give your friends something:

PAMPERING:
You're a guardian angel.

You always keep your friends' well-being in mind. In good times or bad, you're right there. "You're compassionate," explains Biddleman, "and that's why you choose gifts that pamper the body and soul." You always make yourself available to your friends, which means you're the first one to come forward with a ride to the train station or a shoulder to cry on. And this knack for nurturing makes you an indispensable pal!

WHIMSICAL:
You're a fun playmate.

Of course no one is upbeat all the time, but your down days are rare. "Friends look to you when they're feeling glum because they know you'll be a ray of light," says Biddleman. When it's time for gift giving, you love to laugh out loud and go for something wacky. And nothing brings you more happiness than having friends join in the fun.

WEARABLE:
You're a steady sidekick.

You're practically joined at the hip with your friends. "These are completely compatible friendships," explains Biddleman. "You do practically everything together!" Since you know your friends inside and out—from their taste in clothes to their choice of accessories—your gifts are right on target. This kind of intimacy is rare. And your friends treasure it.

MADE BY HAND:
You're a devoted soulmate.

You want your gifts and your friends to last forever—and they do! "You appreciate the effort that goes into creating unique items," says Biddleman. Of course handcrafted gifts are gorgeous—but more important, they're a sign of just how devoted you are!

24. How Polite Are You to Your Friends, Family, Coworkers, Neighbors—Even Strangers?

Do you think you're up on etiquette? Take this quiz and see if you could be the next Miss Manners!

1. **You've just ended your week's stay as a house guest. How do you leave the bed?**
   a. Made up so it looks better than it did the day you first arrived.
   b. With the sheets, pillowcase, and blanket stripped and left in a big heap for the laundry.
   c. With the pillowcase and sheets in a neat pile for the laundry, but the bed covered with the blanket and the pillow placed at the top.

2. **You answer the telephone and the party on the other end says, "Oops, wrong number." What do you say?**
   a. Nothing. Just hang up.
   b. "What number were you trying to reach?"
   c. "That's quite all right."

3. **When should you open and read your mate's mail?**
   a. If it looks like it might be from a secret lover.
   b. If it's addressed to "Occupant."
   c. Never!

4. **You receive a birthday gift from all your friends at the office. Although you've already thanked them in person, will you send a thank-you note, too?**
   a. No—it's not necessary, as long as your gratitude was sincere.
   b. Yes, several—and they will be mailed, individually.
   c. Yes—you will address a thank-you note to the staff and place it on the bulletin board—or send a group e-mail.

5. **What do you consider a good conversation opener?**
   a. Almost anything except, "I've been feeling depressed lately. Let me tell you my woes."
   b. The only polite beginning is to ask, "How are you?
   c. Something that elicits an involved response from the other person.

6. **With proper elevator etiquette in mind, who goes out first?**
   a. Men, so they can hold the door open.
   b. Women and children.
   c. The person nearest the door—only if it's his or her floor.

7. **How would you introduce people who are living together but not married?**
   a. As live-in lovers
   b. As each other's "significant other"
   c. By their names

8. **You prefer to eat your pizza by:**
   a. Ripping it into pieces
   b. Cutting it into bite-size portions with a knife and fork
   c. Lowering it into your mouth by hand, small end of the triangle first

YOUR SCORE

Give yourself 3 points for each "a" answer,
6 points for every "b," and 9 points for each "c."

25. Why Do People Think You're Tops?

21 TO 33 POINTS:
Although you might not mind being impolite, others do.

Good manners open doors to opportunity. Why keep them shut just because you don't care to extend common courtesies? People will appreciate your social graces.

34 TO 51 POINTS:
Generally polite and well mannered, you know how to make a charming impression.

However, when it comes to extending common courtesies to those close to you, you sometimes slip up. Extend the same good manners to loved ones that you do to strangers.

52 POINTS OR MORE:
Move over, Miss Manners!

You could recite the rules of etiquette in your sleep. If people have a question about good manners, they should ask you. Continue being courteous and you'll be an inspiration for future generations.

"Everyone has one or two standout traits that make people love them," says Jan Yager, PhD, author of *Friendshifts*. Take this quiz to discover your special traits, so you can enhance them even more.

1. **A friend says she's feeling really stressed out. You:**
   a. Help her figure out ways to have more time for herself
   b. Get her a gift certificate for a facial or massage
   c. Take her out for a night on the town

2. **If your community was holding an auction to raise money for a new playground, you'd volunteer to:**
   a. Map out a winning strategy for the event
   b. Donate something
   c. Be the auctioneer

3. **When it comes to pets, you have:**
   a. One or none
   b. Three or more
   c. Two

4. **Of these, your favorite de-stressor is:**
   a. Reading a book, watching TV, or enjoying some quiet time
   b. Whipping up a special dinner or batch of cookies
   c. Treating yourself to a manicure or haircut

5. **It's a coworker's birthday. You offer to:**
   a. Pick out a card for everyone to sign
   b. Bake a yummy birthday cake
   c. Organize the gang to go out and celebrate

6. **When a loved one comes to you with a problem, typically you:**
   a. Listen quietly unless you're asked for advice
   b. Ask how you can help and offer a few suggestions
   c. Pick up a little gift to cheer him or her up

YOUR SCORE

NOTE: If your answers fall equally between the two categories, read both descriptions, since you share characteristics of both types.

MOSTLY A'S:
People love you for your WISDOM.

When your friends or family want to know the right thing to do, you're the person they seek out. Fair, honest, and with an intuitive sense of the smartest course to take, you offer advice that truly has the other person's best interest in mind. "What makes you so wise is a balance of confidence, experience, and being grounded in what matters most," says Yager.

MOSTLY B'S:
People love you for your GENEROSITY.

If a friend's car breaks down or she needs last-minute babysitting, you drop everything to come to the rescue. And your loved ones cherish you for it! Generous with not only time but money, you're the first to volunteer. "You get a sense of purpose from giving to those you love, and that makes everyone around you—including you—a winner," says Yager.

MOSTLY C'S:
People love you for your CHARM.

Because you're spontaneous, original, and witty, your friends can't help but love you for your joyous approach to life! "Scientific studies prove optimism is contagious," says Yager. "That's why friends flock to your side." And since you naturally find the silver lining in everything, friends count on you to lift their spirits when they feel down.

26. How Do You Get Your Message Across?

1. **You enroll in a free financial-planning class only to find that the instructor is boring and hard to follow. You:**
   a. Speak to him after class, voicing your concerns and making suggestions
   b. Stop attending, figuring you get what you pay for

2. **While you're at a restaurant with another couple, the pair begins bickering bitterly. To restore peace, you:**
   a. Try to mediate
   b. Break the tension by offering everyone a taste of your dessert

3. **At an office meeting, your boss raises the issue of mandatory overtime, which you oppose. You:**
   a. Speak up. You won't take unfair treatment lying down.
   b. Stay tuned. You'll get the facts, then try to come up with an alternative that will make everyone happy.

4. **A friend asks your opinion of a quilt she's stitching for a contest. After noticing several flaws, you:**
   a. Offer constructive criticism
   b. Focus on the positive

5. **You need a part-time job to help pay off credit card debt. A local café is hiring. Although you have little restaurant experience, you beat out other applicants by:**
   a. Convincing the manager that you'll make up for your lack of experience with hard work
   b. Highlighting any related work experience and creating a sense of calm and competence

6. **Your best friend has put on a few pounds over the holidays. When she asks if you've noticed, you answer:**
   a. "Yes. But everybody gains a little weight at this time of year."
   b. "You look wonderful. You always do."

7. **Lately, your daughter has been dressing like a rock star. To make sure she doesn't embarrass you at a special dinner for the boss, you:**
   a. Let her know you expect to see her in appropriate attire—or else!
   b. Take her on a supervised shopping trip

8. **Your neighbors are hosting a noisy party that shows no signs of stopping and it's well past midnight. You:**
   a. Phone them and politely ask them to quiet down
   b. Turn on some soothing music to try to muffle the noise

YOUR SCORE

NOTE: If your answers fall equally between the two categories, read both descriptions, since you share characteristics of both types.

MOSTLY A'S:
You're upfront and direct.

Nothing gets in your way when you have something to say! Friends, family, and coworkers know they can always count on you to be completely honest. Although your candor may throw some people for a loop, it also keeps the air clean and clear. Thanks to you, everyone can breathe easier.

MOSTLY B'S:
You're subtle and diplomatic.

You prefer to avoid confrontations, opting instead for clever strategies to help smooth over sticky situations. You're so gracious, others may not even realize they're being influenced by you! Your reward: peace of mind and a calm, serene environment.

FAST FACT

WANT TO BE MORE CONVINCING? TRY TO RADIATE WARMTH. RESEARCH SHOWS THIS QUALITY IS KEY TO WINNING PEOPLE OVER TO YOUR WAY OF THINKING!

What makes people grateful for you? "Knowing what makes you special to others is a great confidence booster," says M. J. Ryan, PhD, author of *Attitudes of Gratitude*.

1. **The bouquet that most appeals to you:**
   a. Roses
   b. Orchids
   c. Lavender
   d. Exotic birds of paradise
   e. Wildflowers

2. **Cost aside, which car would you drive?**
   a. Roomy van
   b. Rugged Jeep
   c. Mini Cooper or VW Beetle
   d. Environmentally friendly hybrid
   e. Sports car

3. **Which pastel would you choose to paint your kitchen?**
   a. Pale green
   b. White
   c. Yellow
   e. Peach
   d. Soft blue

4. **What would you do with an extra hour?**
   a. Volunteer in the community
   b. Go shopping
   c. Go out with your closest friends
   d. Catch up with a loved one who lives far away
   e. Work on a hobby or project

5. **Which restaurant would you choose for a bite with the family?**
   a. Chinese
   b. Pizza parlor
   c. Chuck E. Cheese's or another themed spot
   d. A family-style restaurant
   e. A sandwich shop

6. **Which of these romance classics would you love to curl up and watch?**
   a. *Casablanca*
   b. *Gone with the Wind*
   c. *When Harry Met Sally*
   d. *Love Story*
   e. *Breakfast at Tiffany's*

7. **The saying that you're most likely to adopt as your motto is:**
   a. It's better to give than receive.
   b. Still waters run deep.
   c. Smile and the world smiles with you.
   d. True friends are life's greatest gift.
   e. The world is my oyster.

YOUR SCORE

NOTE: If your answers fall equally between the two categories, read both descriptions, since you share characteristics of both types.

MOSTLY A'S:
Your family is grateful for your GENEROSITY.

When someone's in need, you don't wait to be asked for help. You share your prized possessions without batting an eye. "You're tuned into those you love and are happiest when they're happy, too," says Ryan.

MOSTLY B'S:
Your family is grateful for your ROCK-SOLID MIND.

To you, life is a puzzle, and with your strong memory and sharp analytical skills, you enjoy putting all the pieces together. "You love the challenge of gathering information and putting it to good use—and with your excellent judgment, you're a master problem-solver, too," says Ryan.

MOSTLY C'S:
Your family is grateful for your SENSE OF HUMOR.

If laughter is the best medicine, then you're a superhealer! "You inject a little humor—and perspective—into even the tensest situations just when everyone needs it most," says Ryan. Not only does it lift the mood, but research shows laughter is also great for the immune system.

MOSTLY D'S:
Your family is grateful for your LOYALTY.

Once you let someone into your heart, they're in your life to stay—no matter what ups and downs come along. "Steadfast to the core, you stand by your loved ones in the best and worst of times—and make it a point to never judge them," says Ryan.

MOSTLY E'S:
Your family is grateful for your CREATIVITY.

Life is never boring with you around because you add a unique flare to everything! "You're not afraid to take risks or follow where the creative impulse leads—and the results are always truly original," says Ryan.

28. What's the Key to Your Communication Style?

Part One

1. **As the choral director for the school musical, you'll choose the cast by:**
   a. Putting those who can carry a tune in the lead, and the others in the chorus
   b. Holding auditions to find the best singers

2. **Your husband's no Fred Astaire. Nevertheless, what you'd like more than anything for your anniversary is some fun dancing, so you:**
   a. Rent a movie beforehand, such as *Dirty Dancing,* which will make it seem like a wonderful idea
   b. Plan the evening and make it your surprise!

3. **You want your boss to notice all the extra time and effort you've been putting in, so you:**
   a. Leave a routine message on her voice mail
   long after quitting time
   b. Busy yourself near the exit so she see you working away as she leaves

4. **You're dismayed by the fact that your employer doesn't recycle, so you:**
   a. Start collecting for yourself and/or your department
   b. Collect signatures to show company officials how important everyone feels recycling is

Part Two

1. **Honesty isn't always the best policy.**
   Agree_____   Disagree_____

2. **I find it easy to put myself in others' shoes.**
   Agree_____   Disagree_____

3. **The best way to prove a point is by example.**
   Agree_____   Disagree_____

4. **Sending back an entrée at a restaurant is extreme.**
   Agree_____   Disagree_____

YOUR SCORE

NOTE: If your answers fall equally between the two categories, read both descriptions, since you share characteristics of both types.

MOSTLY A'S OR "AGREE"S:
You have soft-spoken savvy.

Charming and persuasive, but never pushy, you've made getting what you want—without ruffling anyone's feathers—into an art! Armed with a keen awareness of what makes people tick, your quiet ways get things done and avert blowups. In fact, your knack for creating calm impresses friends and coworkers alike, which is just one reason you're equally popular at home and at work!

MOSTLY B'S OR "DISAGREE"S:
You have strong convictions.

Never one to pussyfoot around, you cut to the chase and let people know right where you and things, at home or at work, stand—projecting an air of assurance that wins cooperation and respect. You're a firm believer in the phrase "It never hurts to ask," and your requests almost always meet with a positive response because friends, family, and coworkers know they can trust your judgment.

FAST FACT

IF SEATED NEXT TO THE KITCHEN, A RESTAU-RANT, TWO-THIRDS OF US WOULD SPEAK UP AND ASK FOR A BETTER TABLE!

Part One

1. **Friends keep telling me to relax!**
   a. True
   b. False

2. **I've been given a book of inspirational quotes or instant stress-busters as a gift from a coworker or friend.**
   a. True
   b. False

3. **I'd need more than one sheet of paper for a to-do list.**
   a. True
   b. False

4. **I always shop armed with a list (mental or written) and a time limit—browsing just makes me edgy.**
   a. True
   b. False

5. **I can't remember the last time I enjoyed a long soak in the bathtub.**
   a. True
   b. False

6. **I'm always looking at the clock and wondering how it got to be so late.**
   a. True
   b. False

7. **Almost all of the recipes I've clipped in recent months are labeled "easy" or "one dish."**
   a. True
   b. False

Part Two

8. **On your day off, you set the alarm:**
   a. For the usual time
   b. For a later time or not at all

9. **When out-of-town friends visit, you spend the first day:**
   a. Chauffeuring them to local attractions
   b. Catching up on chitchat

10. **Your desk is piled high with papers but you haven't eaten in hours, so you:**
    a. Eat a sandwich at your desk while you work
    b. Take fifteen minutes to munch and relax

11. **While waiting for your morning coffee, you usually:**
    a. Pack lunches, make breakfast, or shower
    b. Read the newspaper or apply makeup

YOUR SCORE

NOTE: If your answers fall equally between the two categories, read both descriptions, since you share characteristics of both types.

MOSTLY "TRUE"S AND A'S:
Your hands are too full!

Phew! Always on the go, go, go, your life is a juggling act of chores and challenges. The phrase "I can't" simply is not in your vocabulary—but with so little room in your routine, you have little or no time for friends. Worse, you could be headed for burnout. Make relaxation and unbreakable dates for socializing a top priority, and you'll be surprised how much "extra" time you can find for ever-important fun!

MOSTLY "FALSE"S AND B'S:
You're cruising comfortably.

Although your life certainly is full, your knack for pacing helps you keep it all under control so that you can have plenty of time for family and friends. When tasks pile up, you decide which duties to delegate and know that to stay cool, calm, and collected; the small stuff may need to be overlooked. After all, what's more important than spending time with those you love?

FAST FACT

WE'RE BUSY, ALL RIGHT! MORE THAN ONE IN FIVE OF US SKIP LUNCH ON ANY GIVEN DAY!

30. Your Favorite Movie Snack Reveals the Kind of Friend You Are!

Everyone knows snacks and movies make a blockbuster combination! But did you know the candy you buy at the concession stand says a lot about what kind of friend you are! It's true! "Research shows there's a real connection between how we treat ourselves and how we treat others," says Susan Burke, RD, of eDiet.com, so pick up your favorite movie munchie—and unwrap the secrets to your popularity!

NACHOS:
You're the life of the party!

"Just like fiery nachos, you're full of spice—there's nothing subtle about your charismatic personality," says Burke. Hot-blooded nacho fanciers love to be the center of attention: you're usually the first on the dance floor and the last to leave the party. It's no wonder friends call you first when they want to have fun! But those who play hard tend to work hard, too, and you're no exception: you keep your nose to the grindstone until the day's work is done—then you gather some friends and get ready to cut loose!

POPCORN:
You're loyal.

"If you pass up all those other, newfangled snacks in favor of this buttery, salty favorite, you possess nostalgic loyalty," says Burke—and that loyalty extends further than popcorn! Friends and family know they can count on you. Your best friend needs emergency child care? You'll be there, even if it means rearranging your schedule. Faithful and true blue, you're loved by one and all—because they know you love them in return!

MILKY WAY:
You're full of surprises.

"Just like these chocolate bars, you're unpredictable and multilayered," says Burke—but it's these traits that make you a sought-after friend. A fun-loving, impulsive risk-taker, you like to throw caution to the wind, and friends get a big kick out of your spunk. Because when they need a push to make a change in their own lives, they look to you, their "let's-go" dynamo, for inspiration!

TWIZZLERS:
You're a kid at heart.

If these sweet licorice whips are still your favorites, then just like Peter Pan, you've never completely grown up. "You approach all your friendships with the same joy you did in childhood," says Burke. Quick to make new friends, happy to forgive when something goes wrong, and content to dream up activities yourself, you make a loyal, fun-loving pal—and that's why you have so many friends who long to spend time with you!

JUNIOR MINTS:
You're super-generous.

"If you get a kick out of these creamy candies, chances are it's because you like to split them with those around you," says Burke—and you're equally generous with your time and energy. The first to

31. What Kind of First Impression Do You Make?

volunteer to sell raffle tickets for a worthy cause, or to organize an office party, you go out of your way to assist your friends in any way. But whether it's with a stress-relieving romp in the snow with your kids or a soothing cup of cocoa before bed, you know how to pamper yourself—so you have the energy to give your all to your buddies!

When people meet you, do you size up favorably—or forgettably? Our quiz reveals all!

1. **If you were applying for a sales position in a high-end department store, what would you wear for your interview?**
   a. A tailored suit with understated earrings and a watch.
   b. A classic suit and a scarf, a necklace, a bracelet, earrings, and an eye-catching belt.
   c. Whatever strikes your fancy that morning—and it probably would be fancy!

2. **Take a good look in the mirror. What best describes your posture?**
   a. Back straight, head high, and arms at side.
   b. Shoulders hunched slightly forward, and head dropped a bit.
   c. Back arched and arms folded in front of your chest.

3. **How often do you polish your nails?**
   a. At least weekly, with occasional touch-ups.
   b. A few times a month.
   c. Every day!

4. **When you meet people for the first time, you make it a point to:**
   a. Greet each one warmly and remember everybody's name
   b. Try to impress by sharing an exciting story of your most recent accomplishment
   c. Assert your opinions, even if they're different from everyone else's

5. **When unexpected guests arrive at your door, what's the first thing you do?**
   a. Offer them some coffee and snacks.
   b. Try to nonchalantly straighten the house.
   c. Suggest they return at a more convenient time.

6. **During the day, how much makeup do you usually wear?**
   a. Just enough to enhance your features and make you look refreshed.
   b. None.
   c. Everything from foundation, blush, and eye shadow to vividly colored lipstick.

YOUR SCORE

NOTE: If your answers fall equally between the two categories, read both descriptions, since you share characteristics of both types.

MOSTLY A'S:
Congratulations! You make a fabulous first impression!

You put your best foot forward by dressing appropriately, listening carefully to conversations, and presenting yourself as a caring, confident person. The secret to your success? It's no secret! Since you're naturally open, honest, and cheerful, you are exactly whom you appear to be. No wonder people look forward to seeing you.

MOSTLY B'S:
You mean well, and most people realize this when they first meet you.

But occasionally your anxiety about new situations makes you feel uncomfortable. To counteract your uneasiness, you may spend too much time talking about yourself—and end up coming across as self-centered. Instead of being so nervous, stand straight, breathe deeply, and let others share their true selves with you.

MOSTLY C'S:
Unfortunately, the first note you strike with new people is usually a little sour.

Instead of wearing what's appropriate for the occasion, you tend to dress to the hilt. Your makeup could also use a little toning down. And rather than make people comfortable, your forthrightness sometimes puts them on the spot. All these tactics are just your way of hiding. You have difficulty meeting strangers, and it takes you a while to build trust. Once you lower your guard, you'll relax and be seen in a better light! Guaranteed!

32. The Secrets Hidden in Your Holiday Party

When it's the season to welcome friends and loved ones into your home—how do you do it? Well, the type of celebration you choose to host reveals secrets about your strongest friendship traits! "The holidays are typically a stressful, busy time, filled with plenty of 'have-to's—so when we do get a choice to do what we want, we tend to plan activities that are easy because they fit best with our natural strengths and preferences," says party-planning veteran Phyllis Cambria, author of *The Complete Idiot's Guide to Throwing a Great Party*. So choose the way you plan to celebrate and discover how you celebrate your friendships, too!

FORMAL DINNER PARTY:
You're a traditionalist.

From the lavish meal you spend hours preparing to the gleaming crystal and china, "a formal dinner party is most often the choice of happy traditionalists who cherish memories of times past," says Cambria. Not for you the casual, devil-may-care lifestyle that seems so prevalent these days: from your salon-styled hair right down to your classic pumps, you believe in taking the time to do things right, whether it's providing a grateful "thanks" when someone does you a favor, a hot meal when your family comes in from the cold, or an honest answer when a friends asks your opinion. You're instilling these solid old-fashioned values in your children—and they're growing up better and happier for it!

AN ALL-AGES EXTRAVAGANZA:
You're a well-loved nurturer.

If nothing says Christmas for you like a huge, multigeneration bash complete with drinks for the grown-ups, Santa for the kids, and a grab bag for all, then odds are you're a popular nurturing mom-type—the kind of person all the neighborhood families know and love! "Women who welcome the challenge of parties like this score high on scale of friendliness and caring, and low on scales of stress," Cambria. Friends look to you as a do-it-all—and you never let them down.

OPEN HOUSE:
You're flexible.

Forget stuffy formal dinners and boring sit-downs—you're happiest just throwing your door open and crying, "Come on over—we'll be here!" "Our research shows that open-house hostesses tend to be easygoing, flexible, and understanding—they love to be surrounded by loved ones, but they dislike strict rules and planning," says Cambria. Friends adore your welcoming, carefree grace—because it's not only your home that's open, but your heart as well.

BRUNCH:
You're a sophisticate.

"Although it's a daytime activity, a holiday brunch can be the most sophisticated of all Christmas get-togethers," says Cambria. "There's something very adult and decadent about indulging in drinks and upscale food during a time when we're supposed to be out getting things done." Of course, you're no slacker, but you love luxuries like expensive perfume or a trip to the salon. And studies show that folks who indulge every so often in the things they crave most are the happiest—so you're in for a very merry holiday, indeed!

COCKTAIL PARTY:
You're a high-energy whiz.

"Those who favor the quick burst of fun that a cocktail party provides tend to be busy, high-energy doers," says Cambria. Naturally active with a low tolerance for boredom, you'd rather be out running errands than lying on the couch. And since studies show those who stay the most active tend to live the longest, pull out that date book and schedule dates with friends and loved ones well into the future!

33. How Do You Express Generosity?

1. **You're going shopping with a few friends to a mall two hours from home. You're more likely to volunteer to:**
   a. Do the driving
   b. Help pay for gas

2. **To support a local charity, you:**
   a. Run their fund-raising drive
   b. Buy a dozen raffle tickets

3. **You're more likely to feel:**
   a. You never have enough money
   b. There's never enough time in the day

4. **When it comes to greeting cards, you usually:**
   a. Make your own. It's more personal that way.
   b. Buy them at a card store. You love the selection.

5. **As a treat for your six-year-old, you:**
   a. Take him on a picnic at the park or beach
   b. Let him choose whatever he wants at the toy store

6. **To celebrate a coworker's promotion, you:**
   a. Invite her over for dinner
   b. Send her a bouquet of flowers

7. **A good friend complains that she's having a hard time losing weight. You help her out by:**
   a. Agreeing to join her on a walk twice a week
   b. Get her an exercise video that sounds easy yet effective

8. **Your mate comes home from work completely stressed out and exhausted. To help him unwind, you:**
   a. Offer to give him a relaxing massage
   b. Take him out to the movies—your treat

9. **Your good buddy is about to give birth to her first baby. You're thrilled and decide to:**
   a. Throw a big shower
   b. Buy her layette

10. **When you read in the newspaper that the humane society is overrun with kittens, it touches you. You:**
   a. Adopt one
   b. Bring over some cartons of cat food

11. **Good neighbors are celebrating their tenth anniversary. You:**
   a. Offer to babysit so they can have a romantic night out
   b. Buy them ten roses, representing each year of their marriage

12. **To reward your daughter for her wonderful end-of-the-year report card, you:**
   a. Take over her chores for a week
   b. Increase her allowance

YOUR SCORE

NOTE: If your answers fall equally between the two categories, read both descriptions, since you share characteristics of both types.

MOSTLY A'S:
You give of yourself.

You always have time, energy, and an open heart for those in need. Friends and family know who to come to when they're having difficulties. You're flexible about time, so you generously offer your services. You volunteer frequently, often working around the clock to get everything accomplished. Because you are creative and caring, your generosity is greatly appreciated.

MOSTLY B'S:
You share what you have.

Although you're not rich, you believe in sharing whatever you have with those you love and those who are less fortunate. Without a second thought, you reach deep into your wallet and give to many causes. You also get pleasure from buying gifts for others. When shopping you often bring home something special for your family and friends. What's your secret? You believe it is far better to give than to receive.

FAST FACT

MORE THAN A THIRD OF US OPEN OUR HEARTS AND OUR POCKETBOOKS TO CHARITY AT LEAST ONCE A MONTH.

PART 3

General Insights

1. Do You Try Too Hard to Please?

If you're like most women, you go out of your way to make sure your loved ones are happy—even if that means stretching yourself too thin. "Women are 80 percent more likely than men to try too hard to please those around them—and feel guilty when they can't," says Jana Kemp, author of *No! How One Simple Word Can Transform Your Life*. Take this quiz and see if you try too hard—and get tips for letting yourself off the hook!

- Rate each question: 1-not necessarily, 2-usually, or 3-always.

1. It's extremely important to be liked by most people.
   1
   2
   3

2. I'll go out of my way to avoid confrontation.
   1
   2
   3

3. I often hear myself saying "I should have" or "I ought to."
   1
   2
   3

4. I'd rather criticize myself than blame others.
   1
   2
   3

5. I often keep my real feelings to myself.
   1
   2
   3

6. At a party, I'm more likely to help the hostess than relax and socialize.
   1
   2
   3

7. I find it difficult to delegate.
   1
   2
   3

8. Compliments make me uncomfortable.
   1
   2
   3

9. I apologize even when I'm right.
   1
   2
   3

10. I frequently have headaches.
    1
    2
    3

YOUR SCORE

Give yourself one point for every 1 selected, two points for every 2, and three points for every 3.

10 TO 15 POINTS:
You have no trouble saying "no"!

With a schedule you stick to like glue, you stay focused on your priorities! Confidant and assertive, you value boundaries in your personal life—which is why you can just as easily say no as say yes. "Balanced types like you experience less work–family conflict and can keep stress at bay because you set up strategies for juggling your many roles," says Kemp. But your type-A personality means you may be a perfectionist—which might mean you have a hard time being flexible. For more flexibility:

- Wait 24 hours before giving an answer to something you're not sure about. Studies show "sleeping on it" helps clarify priorities.
- Find an easy solution. For example, instead of volunteering precious time to a charitable cause, make a donation. Or instead of baking cookies to bring to a bake sale, buy them.
- Use responses that automatically make you more flexible—phrases such as "When I can" or "Maybe in the future" will show you're open to possibilities.

16 TO 20 POINTS:
You're a great juggler!

You can make everyone happy and still manage to find time for yourself. What's your secret for stress-free people-pleasing? "Your strong sense of self allows you to follow your gut reaction, say yes or no, and set priorities with guilt-free confidence," says Kemp. But even the best jugglers face occasional balancing-act challenges. When it happens:

- Delegate. If you can't do something, suggest someone else who can. This way you can stay involved without having to take full responsibility.
- Optimize. When you're at home, turn off your television, radio, cell phone, and e-mail, so that you can be fully present for your family.

21 TO 30 POINTS:
You're the ultimate crowd-pleaser!

Ever wonder why you're always sacrificing? Scientists say it's in your brain! For 60 percent of women, the emotional right side of their brain—the part that makes us more concerned with relationship building—is highly developed. Here are proven ways to overcome the endless "yes" cycle.

- Practice saying no to little things, even if it's just your reflection in the mirror at first. This can give you the confidence to make it a habit.
- Reward yourself once in a while—with stress-free activities such as reading or watching a video. You'll feel more relaxed and learn to put yourself first!

2. Just How Patient with Others Are You?

Do you have loads of calm endurance—or are you more apt to lose your cool? Take this quick quiz to find out!

1. **Of these, the game you most enjoy playing is**
   a. Boggle
   b. Clue
   c. Monopoly

2. **The last dinner you cooked was a:**
   a. Prepared microwave or frozen meal
   b. Family favorite such as spaghetti and meatballs
   c. Brand-new recipe

3. **You usually catch celebrity gossip by:**
   a. Sneaking a peek at magazines at the supermarket checkout
   b. Tuning into such television shows as *Access Hollywood*
   c. Reading tell-all biographies

4. **The birthday cards you give to friends are usually:**
   a. Store bought with a humorous or personal greeting inside
   b. Blank so you can write your own thoughts
   c. Handmade with your own special touches

5. **If you had to take a three-hundred-mile trip, you'd prefer to travel by:**
   a. Plane
   b. Train or bus
   c. Car

6. **You usually take a:**
   a. Quick, vigorous shower.
   b. Ten-minute shower or bath
   c. Long relaxing soak or shower (twenty minutes or more)

7. **You prefer to shop for books, CDs, or DVDs:**
   a. Online
   b. In big discount stores
   c. Browsing small shops

YOUR SCORE

NOTE: If your answers fall equally between the two categories, read both descriptions, since you share characteristics of both types.

MOSTLY A'S:
You hate to wait!

Always on the go, you're a type-A person who's driven to accomplish as much as possible every day. With such a busy life, it's no wonder you get tense when things don't go as planned. "But reacting like this raises stress, increases heart rate, and can even affect your sleep," says Kathleen Hall, author of *A Life in Balance*. Her advice: Take six deep breaths before reacting. Studies confirm this technique cuts stress levels in half!

MOSTLY B'S:
You take things in stride!

Naturally easygoing, you see unexpected snags in your schedule as challenges and enjoy seeking solutions. It's only when you're bored that your patience can run thin, which is why you typically carry a magazine or book with you. "Research shows this is the key to maintaining a happy outlook," says Hall.

3. Do You Have the "Compassion Gene"?

MOSTLY C'S:
You're the calmest of the calm!

You embrace each day and situation as it comes and take a leisurely approach to achieving your goals. Flexibility is at the heart of your patience—you take your time sizing up what's needed and adjust your approach accordingly. "That's why you're a natural teacher—you keep plugging away at explaining things," says Hall.

When it comes to compassion, everybody's different. "Cortiva Institute, a training network for therapeutic massage, created this quiz [which we've adapted] to determine who has what they call the 'compassion gene'," explains institute vice president Jan Schwartz. Find out where you rate on the compassion scale!

1. **If you found a wallet in the street, you'd most likely:**
   a. Look through it for an address to return it yourself
   b. Drop it off at the nearest police precinct and let them handle it
   c. Leave it where it is. Perhaps the person will retrace his or her steps.

2. **You recycle:**
   a. Everything possible
   b. Only when you remember to do it
   c. Just bottles, cans, and papers, if bins are handy

3. **If you're going to be late for an appointment, you:**
   a. Call ahead
   b. Apologize if it's less than twenty minutes; cancel if longer
   c. Try to make up lost time and hope they'll understand

4. **When people want your advice, you most often:**
   a. Offer heartfelt, intuitive advice without holding back
   b. Analyze all the possible solutions using hard facts
   c. Listen to be supportive, even if you don't have the answers

5. **You'd help a friend in need by:**
   a. Bringing flowers or writing cards to cheer her up
   b. Asking what she needs you to do
   c. Offering to pitch in on a specific task you bring up

6. **If you were invited to donate your time at, say, an animal shelter or children's charity, you'd:**
   a. Dive right in—anything to champion such worthy causes
   b. Do it to be social and to learn more
   c. Want to, but find it hard to make the time

YOUR SCORE

NOTE: If your answers fall equally between the two categories, read both descriptions, since you share characteristics of both types.

MOSTLY A'S:
You've got the compassion gene!

Your unusually high level of sensitivity allows you to feel for others and put that empathy into practice. "Your ability to always do the right thing and lend a helping hand—for a loved one or stranger—is an example for the rest of us," says Schwartz. You'd find true happiness from using your innate compassion in humanitarian activities or in a career in the wellness profession.

MOSTLY B'S:
You naturally feel for others.

You're the kind of person who would help someone in need without another thought. Donating your skills or time is natural to you, and you intuitively understand each person's needs. "You are most comfortable taking action, providing real-world solutions," says Schwartz. When your compassion shines through, your self-esteem also gets a boost!

MOSTLY C'S:
You feel others' pain, but you protect yourself, too!

You'd stop at nothing to help your friends and family, but recognize that you need time, too. "Without it, you're likely to overextend yourself, and then you won't be effective in helping others," says Schwartz. You've gained this wisdom the hard way—by taking on too much in the past. Now you make sure you've got time to give it your all, before taking on extra challenges.

4. What Your Favorite Jelly Bean Says about Your Most Appealing Personality Trait!

Admit it: You pick through a bowl of jelly beans to find your favorite flavor. "Everyone does—and according to smell and taste experts, it's because we're drawn to flavors—especially in combination with color—that reflect our strongest personality traits," reveals Adam Decter, CEO of Candy Depot. So, if you love:

LIME: **You're whimsical and playful!**

"Marketing statistics show lime green is the favorite of trendy, fun-loving types—the young and the young at heart," says Decter. It also means:

- You don't believe in the generation gap—which is why your house is the neighborhood hangout for all ages.
- You've got too much on-the-go energy to ever be a couch potato—and doctors say that's the number one prescription for good health!

GRAPE: **You're a creative genius.**

Taste experts say anything in the purple family—from grapes to plums—represents a complex, artistic sensibility. "It's a mix of red's excitement and blue's calm," says Decter. Which is why:

- Studies show you're faster on your feet than most— always ready with a witty remark or a quick decision!
- You're more psychic than most—which is why you always check your horoscope.

LICORICE: **You're a maverick.**

Not everyone goes for the unique flavor of licorice, but "those who do tend to be forward-thinking individualists," says Decter. Trailblazers like you also:

- Set goals well in advance, which psychologists say is the mark of a true leader!

- Thrive on new experiences, finding ways to vary life at every turn.
- Rate high on scales of self-confidence.

STRAWBERRY: **You're fueled by optimism.**

"Our research shows people who are drawn to strawberry tend to be upbeat types," say Decter. You're also:

- More likely to achieve your goals, since studies show you focus on the positive and don't give up!
- Grateful—and psychologists say counting your blessings is the key to contentment.

CHERRY: **You're a born romantic.**

"Surveys show cherry-jelly-bean lovers tend to be charming, romantic types who measure high in sensuality and femininity," says Decter. Along with a love-conquers-all philosophy:

- Studies show you're an extrovert who puts your feelings right out there for all to see.
- You're intense, impulsive, and burning with energy.

FAST FACT

THE DIFFERENCE BETWEEN A GOURMET AND TRADITIONAL JELLY BEAN? GOURMET BEANS ARE SMALLER AND SOFTER, AND HAVE FLAVOR IN THE SHELL AND CENTER. TRADITIONAL BEANS CONTAIN FLAVORS IN THE SHELL ONLY!

5. Discover Your Most Admired Quality the Next Time You Eat Out!

Next time you and your family head out for ethnic food, take notice: where you go reveals a lot! "After years of study, scientists have conluded that people's preferences for different types of food are based 50 percent on flavor—and 50 percent on the mental association we have with them," says psychotherapist Ellen Forman, PhD. (An example? Home-cooked comfort food, such as meat loaf and mashed potatoes—most folks enjoy it as much for its childhood association with safety and love as they do for its flavor.) "That's why, by examining your favorite type of food, we gain insight into your personality," she explains. So pick your favorite ethnic food from our menu—and find out why you really are what you eat!

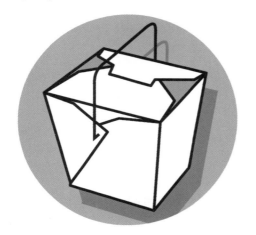

CHINESE:
You're a resourceful leader.

Researchers found that folks who rank Chinese food their favorite tend to be strong-willed leaders who know what they want without needing input from others. A resourceful leader with a drive to win, chances are you're climbing the ladder of success almost effortlessly. And you're lucky in another way: studies show that folks who "know their mind" tend to have lower blood pressure and fewer heart attacks!

JAPANESE:
You're an orderly achiever.

"Japanese food is a precise, delicate cuisine that appeals to people who appreciate detail and run their lives in an organized, goal-oriented way," says Forman. No jumbled piles of paper for you: keeping things neat helps you think clearly! Your high-achieving secret? You stick to a routine, keep your date book up-to-the-minute, and wake up early to make every day the best it can be!

ITALIAN:
You're a big-hearted social butterfly!

Nothing says "family" (or friends getting together) like traditional family fare, which for centuries has been associated with open-armed, everyone's-welcome, family-style dining. "Indeed, studies show folks who prefer it tend to be warm, social extroverts who get along well with others," says Forman. Whether you're heading out for Sunday dinner with a loved one or throwing a bash for fifty friends, you're in your element when you're surrounded by people—and you attract friends like bees flock to, well, tomato sauce!

MEXICAN:
You're a fiery adventurer.

According to experts, folks who enjoy this spicy,over-the-top cuisine have a fire burning in their soul! "These subjects rate high on scales of risk-taking and originality and have an extremely low tolerance for boredom," say Forman. With your thirst for thrilling excitement, you're not afraid to explore new territory—and you're ready to conquer the world!

INDIAN:
You're an even-keeled peacemaker.

No other cuisine is as much about give-and-take as Indian food: it's fiery curries are balanced with cool, soothing yogurt sauces or sweet chutneys. "Likewise, studies show those who enjoy this yin-yang approach tend to be even-keeled peacemakers, who appreciate balance in their life," says Forman. It's this sensible attitude that helps you achieve your goals—and makes you such a success!

FAST FACT:

AMERICANS GOBBLE UP A WHOPPING 3 BILLION PIZZAS EVERY YEAR—SIGNIFICANTLY MORE THAN THE ITALIANS DO!

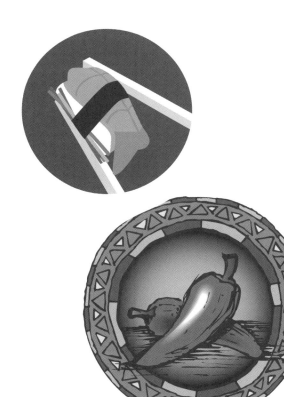

6. What Color Is Your Toothbrush?
It Reveals Secrets about Your Approach to Life!

Of course, we all pick a new toothbrush every few months—so what's news about that? Well, recent research proves the color you choose reveals secrets about your current state of mind! "Scientific studies prove our preference for color is primal; it lies hidden deep within our psyches and reflects our real moods, feelings, and desires," says color researcher Leatrice Eiseman, author of *Colors for Your Every Mood*. So pick the hue that goes with your pearly whites—and discover what makes you smile!

PURPLE: You're feeling creative.

Purple is often the favorite color of artists, performers, writers, and mystics—creative people who are guided by their heart, not their head. "A sudden preference for purple shows you're moving through a creative period where you may reject conformity and convention," say Eiseman. So have fun with yourself—your new willingness to let your creative vision shine through proves you're no shrinking violet!

GREEN: You're feeling generous.

Traditionally, green is not only the color of money but also a sign of generosity and growth. When you're attracted to green, you're feeling generous with your time, money, and emotions," says Eiseman. In fact, surveys reveal that green lovers tend to be innate do-gooders who go out of their way to make the world a better place. And just like the green of the trees and the grass, your goodness continues to grow!

RED: You're feeling dynamic!

"Over and over, color scientists have shown that red—the highest arc of the rainbow—appeals to those with passionate, dynamic temperaments," explains Eiseman. And if you choose it now, odds are you're experiencing an unusual surge of boldness! Like the red badge of courage, your fiery demeanors means that now is your time! So apply for that promotion, brave that advanced yoga class, try that bold new hair color: since red lovers are energetic, intense achievers, you can't lose! In other words, you have what it takes to make your dreams come true!

YELLOW: You're feeling joyful!

The color of sunny days, daffodils, and lemonade, "yellow traditionally signals joy and friendship," says Eiseman—so it's no wonder that in studies correlating color and mood, yellow is associated with comedy, happiness, and playfulness! If it's your current choice, chances are you've been experiencing a surge of bright optimism that attracts others to you. Your upbeat, fun-loving attitude makes everyone's day a little brighter!

BLUE: You're feeling stressed!

It's the color of deep blue skies and crystal-clear lakes, so it came as no surprise to scientists who found that blue actually reduces heartbeat, blood pressure, and respiration! "If your drawn to this color, your subconscious is probably longing for relaxation," says Eiseman. So spend an evening playing games with the kids, sharing a quiet dinner with your partner, or indulging in a soothing half hour in the tub. Your body and soul will thank you for it!

7. Are You Young at Heart?

Looking at the world through a child's eyes can sometimes make life more fun! Find out if you're still in touch with your youthful self.

1. **You're strolling on the boardwalk when you spot a merry-go-round, one of your favorite childhood rides. You:**
   a. Pass it by. Who wants to wait in line with a bunch of kids?
   b. Watch others enjoy it
   c. Don't hesitate to buy a ticket and climb on!

2. **To celebrate your anniversary, you plan to:**
   a. Spend a quiet evening at home
   b. Go out for a special dinner with your significant other
   c. Throw a big bash and invite all your friends

3. **Your favorite newspaper section is:**
   a. The international news
   b. The gossip column
   c. The comics

4. **For weekend wear, you prefer:**
   a. A slightly more casual version of your work wear
   b. Jeans and a T-shirt
   c. Something trendy and fun

5. **When teenagers kiss on the street, you think:**
   a. "What inappropriate behavior."
   b. "I used to do that."
   c. "I wish my husband were here!"

YOUR SCORE

Give yourself 3 points for each "a" answer, 6 points for every "b," and 9 points for each "c."

15 TO 24 POINTS:
Stuck in your ways, you never quite let loose.

Try spending some time with children, and let them show you how to be more playful. You'll be surprised at how much fun it can be.

25 TO 34 POINTS:
You have a playful spirit.

You always like to join in the fun, but you know better than to neglect the more serious side of life. Lucky you! You get to enjoy the best of both worlds.

35 POINTS OR MORE:
A child in almost every way, you sometimes carry this mind-set just a little too far.

Although it's great to be young at heart, don't lose sight of the lessons age has taught you.

8. How Mysterious Are You?

1. **You prefer clothing that:**
   a. Shows off your curves
   b. Conceals your figure

2. **You coworker's last remark hurt your feelings. You:**
   a. Talk to her about it immediately
   b. Mull it over in your journal

3. **Which feature do you emphasize most with makeup?**
   a. Depends on my mood
   b. Eyes

4. **Your party guests are raving about your specialty dish. You respond by:**
   a. Sharing the recipe
   b. Offering a gracious thanks and remaining humble

5. **You consider yourself a better:**
   a. Conversationalist
   b. Listener

6. **You'd prefer to live in a house with:**
   a. Lots of windows and open spaces
   b. Plenty of cozy rooms

7. **When dining out, you'll feel most comfortable seated at a table:**
   a. Right in the middle of the room
   b. Tucked off to the side or in a corner

8. **Your hairstyle is:**
   a. Simple and swept off your face
   b. Layered with bangs

9. **Imagine a work of art based on the colors in your wardrobe. Your masterpiece is:**
   a. A bright canvas splashed with cheery, upbeat colors
   b. An evocative black-and-white photograph

10. **Your circle of friends is:**
    a. Wide and encompassing
    b. Small but close-knit

11. **You're going to an old-fashioned Halloween party. When choosing a costume, you ask yourself:**
    a. "Who do I want to be?"
    b. "What's the most complete disguise?"

12. **Have you told your best friend your deepest, darkest secret?**
    a. Yes, but only part of the story.
    b. No.

YOUR SCORE

NOTE: If your answers fall equally between the two categories, read both descriptions, since you share characteristics of both types.

MOSTLY A'S:
You're still full of surprises.

Because you project such a sunny persona, friends and family probably feel they know you through and through—at first. Gradually, however, they've probably come to realize that however much they can rely on your love and support, your ideas and reactions may not be as predictable! From random acts of kindness to unexpected favors, your special brand of surprise is the kind that always delights!

MOSTLY B'S:
You're an intriguing puzzle.

You're very modest—so much so, you may not be aware of the cloud of mystery surrounding you! Unassuming and humble, you'd rather listen to what others have to say than reveal your accomplishments—and this reticence leaves others with a question mark in their minds. This "q" factor can give you the upper hand—because you possess the element of surprise!

FAST FACT

DID YOU KNOW NEXT TO A GOOD LOVE STORY, WE ENJOY A MYSTERY MOST: MYSTERY NOVELS ARE THE SECOND MOST POPULAR BOOK GENRE!

1. **To put your husband in the mood for romance, you:**
   a. Greet him at the door wearing something alluring
   b. Serve his favorite meal

2. **Everything in your life is looking up—unfortunately, your best friend's life seems to be headed in the opposite direction. When talking to her, you:**
   a. Hope your high spirits are contagious
   b. Downplay your good fortune

3. **You feel the best way to deal with conflict is to:**
   a. Confront issues head on and resolve them before they grow
   b. Consider the other person's point of view and try to bend

4. **Your favorite niece is getting married. At her bridal shower, you:**
   a. Meet and greet
   b. Help decorate

5. **When it come to jewelry, you like to wear:**
   a. Large, glittering stones that usually garner compliments
   b. Subtle, understated pieces that accent your wardrobe

6. **If you wanted to set a stranger at ease, you'd:**
   a. Smile your widest
   b. Look, listen, and nod

7. **On a scale of 1 to 10, how punctual are you?**
   a. 5, 6, or 7
   b. 9 or 10

8. **How do you think your coworkers see you?**
   a. Assertive and outgoing
   b. Modest, reliable, and efficient

9. **Your friend is sharing an idea she has for decorating her bedroom. You're not that fond of it, so you:**
   a. Say, "How creative!" then tactfully work in some of your misgivings
   b. Say something neutral, such as "That sounds interesting"

10. **If you were the boss, you'd be seen as:**
    a. Someone who can handle power and fairness
    b. A mother hen who takes care of her underlings

11. **To help sponsor a community playground or garden, you'd:**
    a. Organize a fund-raiser; you'll be the mistress of ceremonies
    b. Donate some of your cash (anonymously)

YOUR SCORE

NOTE: If your answers fall equally between the two categories, read both descriptions, since you share characteristics of both types.

MOSTLY A'S:
You're naturally radiant.

There's an unmistakable glow about you! You're outgoing, spontaneous, and bubbling with enthusiasm, and people are instinctively drawn to you and feel inspired by your company. With your dazzling smile, bouncy wit, and extraordinary flair for conversation, your confidence is as contagious as it is engaging. Whether you're charming the boss or the supermarket checkout clerk, your inimitable warmth makes you Miss Popularity!

MOSTLY B'S:
You're a hidden jewel.

You charm others not by getting attention but by making people feel good about themselves. Ever thoughtful, attentive, and considerate, you're always ready to lend a helping hand or a listening ear. You never forget a face or a name, and your consideration endears you to one and all.
It's no wonder you tend to keep friends for life—and draw new ones into your circle without even trying!

FAST FACT

FROWNING REQUIRES 72 FACIAL MUSCLES, WHEREAS IT TAKES ONLY 14 TO SMILE!

10. The Personality Clues in Your Salad!

It's no toss-up! Most of us agree: the best part of a salad is the dressing! But did you know the dressing that covers your greens actually reveals the real you? It's true! "While observing hundreds of focus groups, we've discovered that there's a clear connection between salad dressing choice and personality traits we unconsciously project to others," confirms Ali Tadlaoui of Wishbone and Western Salad Dressings. So choose your favorite salad topper—and find out why nothing tops you!

ITALIAN:
You're a daring doer.

Robust and spicy, with a bit of a kick: if this describes your salad dressing, it also describes you! "Those who enjoy zesty Italian dressing tend to look for 'zest' in other areas of life as well: they're daring, outgoing, and adventurous," says Tadlaoui. With your high-flying flair and brave spirit, you're the first to try a bold nail color (purple sparkles, anyone?) or take a spur-of-the-moment trip to someplace warm and tropical! Your motto? "It can't hurt to try"—and that's the attitude that puts you in the winner's circle!

THOUSAND ISLAND:
You're a social butterfly.

Thousand Island is the most popular dressing at parties—and "industry surveys show most folks who love its sweet, tangy taste say it reminds them of good times!" says Tadlaoui. (No wonder it's most popular down South, where hospitality is the order of the day!) Chances are, you're a charming extrovert who positively shines anywhere you get the chance to be social! You're happiest when you're surrounded by those you love: chatting at a dinner party or even just telling your little ones a bedtime story! Loved ones near and far look forward to being with you—because your outgoing nature means a guaranteed great time!

RANCH:
You're a kid at heart!

Surveys show ranch is America's number one dressing—because it's the most popular among kids who love its creamy buttermilk flavor. "And grown women who pick it as their favorite also tend to retain some childlike characteristics, scoring in the top percentiles for playfulness and love of indulgences," says Tadlaoui. Because you're responsible yet delightfully unpredictable, pals know that when you're around there's never a dull moment—and that's why your social calendar is always full!

FRENCH:
You're an old-fashioned nurturer!

With its tart vinegar and mild herbs, French dressing is the epitome of fancy French food. Yet "surprisingly, our studies show those who choose it are the most likely to embrace down-home American values like patriotism and honesty," says Tadlaoui. Hardworking and loyal, you raise your family with the same values your mother did: you care for your children with loving discipline, keep a clean home, and try to have a hot meal ready on a cold night. With your practical outlook and sensible advice, you're as American as apple pie—even if you do like a little French accent now and then.

11. Which of These European Cities Would You Love to Visit?

Your Destination Reveals Your Most Basic Values!

Imagine you've won a free ticket to your choice of one of these glamorous, romantic European cities. Travel experts say the city you choose says a lot about who you are! "We've found that tourists pick cities that remind them of their own childhood and heritage—places that reflect their most basic values," says Alexis Rochefort of the Institute of Certified Travel Agents. So pick your perfect place and find out where you're really at!

PARIS:
You're a dynamic leader.

It's the alluring City of Lights—and it's jam-packed with more must-see attractions, must-taste restaurants, and must-shop stores than any other European city! "Enjoying all that Paris has to offer means diving in with a well-thought-out plan of attack—and if you rise to the occasion, you're a self-starter who gets right out there and enjoys everything life throws your way!" says Rochefort. Just like the French who are known for elegance, feistiness, and wit, you're a charismatic, take-charge leader.

LONDON:
You're a traditionalist!

From the pomp and pageantry of Buckingham Palace to the timeless afternoon ritual of tea and crumpets, everything about London says deep tradition—and that's what you love about it! "Like the city itself, your roots run deep: you've got strong ties to your family and community, and you hold tight to time-tested values," says Rochefort. Regarded as a pillar of your community, you do things the old-fashioned way, whether it's knowing the names of every single one of your kid's friends or stashing away a chunk of each paycheck instead of spending it!

VIENNA:
You adore the finer things!

Elegant Vienna is famous for its soaring cathedral spires, majestic formal gardens—and decadent, indulgent desserts. "Vienna is a hold over from a more refined era, and if you long to be part of it, you have a true appreciation for culture, manners, and luxury,"

says Rochefort. From your sparkling dinner parties to the fresh flowers that adorn your dining table, everything you do says grace and elegance! Your appreciation for the finer things makes everyone's life a little less ordinary—and they love you for it!

COPENHAGEN:
You love the simple life!

Flashy and complicated? Not Copenhagen! Filled with practical, down-to-earth calm, this relaxed city is the perfect place to dress down, stroll around, and share the simple life of its famously friendly people. "Like the Danes, you tend to shrug off the latest 'must-have' trends, valuing deeper experiences far more than appearance and putting practicality above all else!" says Rochefort.

VENICE:
You're wise!

Picture it: you and your husband ensconced in an old-fashioned gondola, gliding down a narrow Venetian canal as you gaze into each other's eyes. "Venice is a romantic city where visitors are encouraged to relax, unwind, and truly appreciate their companions," says Rochefort. If it's your idea of heaven, you know that the best things in life are those that can't be bought or counted: true love, quiet contemplation, and time to appreciate your home and family.

12. Discover Your Star Quality!

According to a new survey, these five Hollywood hunks are the ones American women find the most attractive. But did you know there's a reason beyond good looks that makes you admire the movie star you do? "Research shows we identify with the celebrity who shares the same type of charisma that we value in ourselves," says relationship expert Jill Spiegel. So pick your big-screen heartthrob—and discover your own star quality.

GEORGE CLOONEY:
You're a fun-loving mystery woman!

What makes women swoon at the sight of George Clooney? "It's partly his good looks and fun-loving attitude—but also his sense of mystery underneath. We sense there's more to him than he lets on," says Spiegel. Like Clooney, you're a natural jokester who loves to play—and you're drawn to his mysterious side because you have one of your own! A natural at parties, you shine in the spotlight—and one on one, you're a charismatic charmer!

RUSSELL CROWE:
You're a flexible overachiever!

Russell Crowe is more than just a pretty face: he's a chameleon-like actor who's flexible enough to tackle any role. If he's your choice, chances are you're also an overachiever who excels in many roles, from wife to friend to mom. Unafraid to try new things, you pursue your dreams with gusto!

BRAD PITT:
You're a true-blue girl next door!

He's the all-American boy: blond and blue-eyed— and he's got the kind-hearted personality to match! "If you're attracted to Brad Pitt's down-to-earth nature, odds are you've got a girl-next-door tendency yourself," says Spiegel. Friendly and loyal, you're happiest when you're surrounded by family and loved ones.

SEAN CONNERY:
You're strong and resourceful.

No matter what the role, Sean Connery always projects a tough yet sensitive image: he's a powerful, calming force in a sea of strife. "Women who admire him tend to be highly organized and creatively resourceful," say Spiegel. But just like Sean Connery, your no-nonsense exterior hides a heart of gold!

PAUL NEWMAN:
You're a generous go-getter.

Paul Newman was not only a classic screen idol but a renowned philanthropist as well: his food company, Newman's Own, donates its profits to charity! "Likewise, surveys show that what appeals to women who admire him was his generous spirit and real-world stability—he was married to Joanne Woodward for over forty years," Spiegel notes. Like him, you give your all to help others without expecting anything in return. You live by the golden rule—and your care and concern come back to you tenfold!

FAST FACT

WHAT ACTOR DO MEN ADMIRE MOST?
CLINT EASTWOOD!

13. Are You an Approval Junkie?

Sure, all of us want to be liked. But if you're sacrificing your values and self-respect for the sake of a little apple-polishing, perhaps it's time to take a closer look …

1. **Your friend is head over heels in love with a guy who couldn't care less. You:**
   a. Tell her the truth and suffer the consequences
   b. Beat around the bush and drop a few hints
   c. Pretend he's a prince

2. **As a child, you were known most as:**
   a. Little Angel
   b. Bossy Brat
   c. Daring Daredevil

3. **Your mate adores you in red, but you think it makes you look like Fire Engine Number 9. You:**
   a. Act alarmed—and refuse to wear it
   b. Ring his bells and wear red anytime
   c. Wear red only to bed and spark some passion!

4. **At a dinner party, you find you disagree with your host's views on practically everything. You:**
   a. Sulk
   b. Walk out in a huff
   c. Smile and nod

5. **Your beau boasts he's the best bowler in town. At the alley, you:**
   a. Knock his socks off by knocking down the pins without appearing to try
   b. Roll your ball into the gutter—on purpose
   c. Just play your best

6. **What would you do if your boss made sexual advances?**
   a. Suffer in silence
   b. Ask him to stop
   c. Report him at once!

7. **Your in-laws are constantly criticizing your cooking. You:**
   a. Try harder to improve your cuisine
   b. Oops! *Accidentally* spill gravy on their laps
   c. Make reservations at a local restaurant

8. **You let an elderly woman go ahead of you in the grocery line. Now a child with one item asks if she can cut in, too. You:**
   a. Tell her you'd like to let her but you're in a rush
   b. Wave her ahead
   c. Say, "Age before beauty, my dear"

Part Two

1. **I've always been popular.**
   Agree_____ Disagree_____

2. **Pride is not a quality I cultivate.**
   Agree_____ Disagree_____

3. **It's hard to say no.**
   Agree_____ Disagree_____

4. **I try not to be the bearer of bad news.**
   Agree_____ Disagree_____

5. I do anything to avoid arguments.

Agree_____ Disagree_____

YOUR SCORE

- Give yourself the following number of points for each answer:

  1. a-3, b-5, c-7
  2. a-3, b-7, c-5
  3. a-3, b-7, c-5
  4. a-5, b-3, c-7
  5. a-3, b-7, c-5
  6. a-7, b-5, c-3
  7. a-7, b-3, c-5
  8. a-5, b-7, c-3

- For Part Two, give yourself 3 points for each statement with which you agree.

- Add the scores from Parts One and Two.

39 POINTS OR LESS:
Supremely self-confident, you don't give a hoot what anyone else thinks.

You frankly don't care if people talk behind your back or put you down right to your face. This sort of independence is admirable to a point, but sometimes caution and compromise are more appropriate. We know you want to get your point across—but is unpopularity worth the price? Try to use some diplomacy, but do continue to buck the system. It's individuals like you who can change the world!

40 TO 55 POINTS:
When you feel strongly about something, you stick to your guns, even if your efforts backfire.

You're tough and can take the heat of disapproval without melting. You're especially upfront with your family, friends, and coworkers. But when it comes to romance, you lose all conviction. You so desperately want the man in your life to think you're the answer to his dreams that you present whatever picture he wants to see. You're likely to have more success if you stop trying too hard. It's the real you who will win his heart, not the one who begs for approval.

56 POINTS OR MORE:
If you had your way, every time you uttered a word it would win a round of applause.

You want nothing more than to be accepted by everyone. That's why to be in favor, you'll say or do just about anything. Conviction is an empty word in your vocabulary. Underneath your unceasing drive for popularity is a women who won very little acceptance as a child. Now you want to make up for lost time. But the words "To thine self be true" should be taken to heart. You've got a lot going for you. Trust yourself and you can lead the way!

14. Who Should Play You On Screen?

The Answer Gives You "Reel" Insights!

Your favorite celebs aside, if you were casting someone to play you, who might best capture your true essence on screen? Our quiz, with the help of Maria Grace, PhD, author of *Reel Fulfillment*, will lead you to the perfect match—and reveal insights about how you see yourself!

1. **The time of day when you usually feel your best is:**
   a. Morning
   b. Evening
   c. Afternoon

2. **You'd welcome newcomers to the neighborhood with:**
   a. A plate of homemade chocolate chip cookies
   b. A bottle of wine
   c. An offer to help them unpack

3. **You drink your morning cup of coffee or tea from:**
   a. A special mug
   b. A take-out cup from your favorite coffee shop
   c. Any mug within reach

4. **You most enjoy shopping for:**
   a. Fun accessories such as watches or belts
   b. Shoes
   c. A sweater

5. **The lipstick color you wear most often is:**
   a. Light and subtle (pink, rose, peach)
   b. Bright and rich (red, plum, cranberry)
   c. Clear or neutral (beige or a gloss)

6. **You'd use an extra half hour at lunch to:**
   a. Make phone calls to friends or family members
   b. Shop
   c. Take a walk

7. **When you want to relax at home, you throw on:**
   a. Sweatpants
   b. Pretty pajamas
   c. Your favorite jeans and T-shirt

YOUR SCORE

NOTE: If your answers fall equally between the two categories, read both descriptions, since you share characteristics of both types.

MOSTLY A'S:
You should be played by CAMERON DIAZ!

Cameron Diaz, with her good-hearted, girl-next-door on-screen persona, would be perfectly cast as you in your life story! "Diaz comes across as genuine and approachable, and like her, you're someone who makes everything you touch a little brighter," says psychologist Grace. Just like Diaz, your fun, free-spirited nature and undying loyalty make your popularity soar!

MOSTLY B'S:
You should be played by CATHERINE ZETA-JONES!

Your radiant combination of glamour, elegance, and inner strength makes Catherine Zeta-Jones the perfect star to play you! "Like Zeta-Jones, you're a woman who knows what she needs and wants and isn't afraid to use all the charm at her disposal to make it happen," says Grace.

153

MOSTLY C'S:
You should be played by KIRSTEN DUNST!

When the going gets tough, you rely on your intelligence and wit and steadfast resolve to put you back on top—just like the characters Kirsten Dunst typically plays. "You share Dunst's optimism, courage, and determination," says Grace. Not to mention the belief that if you give your all to something, you'll shine In the end!

FAST FACT

CAMERON DIAZ WAS DISCOVERED BY A PHOTOGRAPHER AT A HOLLYWOOD BASH, WHO HELPED HER SIGN WITH A PRESTIGIOUS MODELING AGENCY!

Do you believe in magic? Surveys show that for most of us, angels, fairies, unicorns, and other mystical creatures evoke powerful feelings of awe, wonder, and calm—but there's more to it than that! It turns out that the fantasy creature you're most drawn to represents the quality that friends most admire in you—the magical essence that makes you who you are! "Personality studies show that subconsciously, we're each drawn to the particular creature that embodies the strongest quality we project to the outside world," explains Connie Kaplan, DMIM, author of Dreams Are Letters from the Soul. So, which do you prefer?

ANGELS:
Your magical quality is compassionate caring.

We all wish we had a guardian angel, but your loved ones really do have one—it's you! "Folks who identify most strongly with angels often boast some of their same characteristics: the ability to aid without interfering, the desire to do good as a means of feeling good, and the compassion to come to the rescue of those in need," says Kaplan. Tenderhearted and outraged by injustice, you get a real sense of joy from working behind the scenes to help others. A whopping 85 percent of Americans believe in angels—and the proof is right in the mirror!

MERMAIDS:
Your magical quality is good-natured charm!

"Throughout history, mermaids have been portrayed as alluring, happy, and slightly mischievous," says Kaplan—and those who identify with them tend to be charismatic and brimming with good-natured humor.

A natural at parties and social gatherings, you entice friends with your bright, easygoing wit—and because you feel supremely comfortable in your own skin, admirers practically fall at your feet (er, your tail)!

FAIRIES:
Your magical quality is youthful joie de vivre.

Surveys show that those who are entranced by fairies tend to be cheerful extroverts who've never lost their youthful joie de vivre. Sure, you've got responsibilities, but you always find time for a game of hide-and-seek with the kids because it makes you feel just as exhilarated as it does them! You jump into fun with both feet—and it's this attitude that keeps you vibrant: studies show those who have the most new experiences age the least!

UNICORNS:
Your magical quality is gentle diplomacy.

"Traditionally, the role of these gentle, loving creatures is to maintain the universe as a balanced, harmonious whole," says Kaplan—and that's why you're so drawn to them! Sensitive, diplomatic, and insightful, you're the one friends come to for practical advice—and you're always right on target! What's your secret? Your spectacular intuition! It helps you pick up on body language and inflection so you can assess any situation in a flash!

DRAGONS:
Your magical quality is bold confidence.

"In ancient times, the dragon was seen as both a powerful warrior and an awesome force to be reckoned with—a symbol of unrivaled bravery," says Kaplan.

And surveys show that those who choose it over gentler fantasy creatures do so because that's how they see themselves: as bold, confident conquerors who go after what they want with vigor! So whether you're running for town council or committing to a weight-loss program, you chase your bright future with a fire-breathing zest that virtually guarantees success!

16. Can You Resist Temptation?

Do you ever:

1. **Keep an open box of candy in your house for more than a week without eating it all?**
   a. Often
   b. Rarely

2. **Resist spreading a tidbit of gossip you've heard?**
   a. Often
   b. Rarely

3. **Spend the whole day at a mall without buying a single thing?**
   a. Often
   b. Rarely

4. **Stick firmly to your TV time limit, even when your kids are begging for more?**
   a. Often
   b. Rarely

5. **Keep a surprise party or a gift a secret?**
   a. Often
   b Rarely

6. **Stop yourself from telling a friend a movie's ending because she hasn't seen it yet?**
   a. Often
   b. Rarely

7. **Quit a bad habit like smoking, eating junk food, or nail-biting, by going cold turkey?**
   a. Often
   b. Rarely

8. **Go grocery shopping for the week and buy only what's on your list?**
   a. Often
   b. Rarely
9. **Finish a crossword puzzle without looking up the answers in the dictionary?**
   a. Often
   b. Rarely
10. **Put leftovers away without sneaking another bite?**
   a. Often
   b. Rarely

11. **Walk away from an item you really love because it is just too expensive?**
   a. Often
   b. Rarely

12. **Stop yourself from reminding your husband to do a chore?**
   a. Often
   b. Rarely

YOUR SCORE

NOTE: If your answers fall equally between the two categories, read both descriptions, since you share characteristics of both types.

MOSTLY A'S:
You have natural willpower.

Once you set your mind to something, temptation doesn't have a chance. Whether you decide to quit a bad habit, keep a secret, or stick to a routine, you do it with a will of steel. This strength of character stems from your strong and independent nature. But that doesn't mean you're unyielding—

when a situation calls for rethinking or compromise, you're easily able to make positive changes.

MOSTLY B'S:
You take one step at a time.

Small steps, rather than giant leaps, are likely to bring you success. Eventually, you accomplish every goal you set for yourself. If, on occasion, a temptation wins out, it's no big deal. You know that tomorrow is another day and you'll begin again. Your realistic attitude is to be applauded. You not only manage to follow through with your plans, but you do it with as little stress as is possible.

FAST FACT

MORE THAN 40 PERCENT OF PEOPLE POLLED GIVE INTO TEMPTATION DAILY WITH A "TASTE" FROM SOMEONE ELSE'S PLATE!

17. Discover Your Car Type and Find Out What Drives You!

Forget about what you're currently driving—if money were no object, which car would suit the real you? "There are personality traits that match different car models," says Tom Appel, editor of Consumer Guide Automotive. Discover yours!

1. **The '70s sitcom you'd enjoy seeing again would be:**
   a. *The Mary Tyler Moore Show*
   b. *The Partridge Family*
   c. *One Day at a Time*

2. **If you had a flat tire, you'd:**
   a. Call AAA or a local garage to have it fixed
   b. Put on your emergency lights and wait for someone to stop
   c. Grab the spare and car tools and see if you could do it yourself

3. **The sofa style that you like best is:**
   a. Sleek and contemporary
   b. Overstuffed and shabby chic
   c. A sectional recliner

4. **Your favorite handbag is:**
   a. An expensive-looking designer (or knockoff) bag
   b. An adorable little clutch
   c. A roomy tote with a lot of pockets

5. **Which of these tempting desserts would be the toughest for you to resist?**
   a. Tiramisu
   b. A gooey hot fudge sundae
   c. Warm apple cobbler with a dollop of whipped cream

6. **The Hollywood hunk you'd love to have dinner with is:**
   a. Brad Pitt
   b. Johnny Depp
   c. Harrison Ford

7. **When you want to remember an appointment you:**
   a. Immediately put it in your daily scheduler
   b. Scribble it on the nearest piece of paper
   c. Jot it on the kitchen calendar in red

YOUR SCORE

NOTE: If your answers fall equally between the two categories, read both descriptions, since you share characteristics of both types.

MOSTLY A'S:
You'd have a convertible, such as a Mustang!

"Convertibles like the Mustang promise a sense of freedom," says Appel. So, they're the perfect match for independent types who enjoy the finer things in life and work hard for everything they get. Like the car, your personality is daring—you always speak your mind and take risks because you like the rewards it gets you.

MOSTLY B'S:
You'd have a fun car, such as a Mini Cooper!

Offbeat and creative, you'd happily swap practicality for the promise of spontaneity and unknown possibilities. "Cute, sassy, and feminine, this car defines a lively personality that's always on the go and hates to be held back," says Appel.

MOSTLY C'S:
You'd have a practical car, such as a Prius!

According to a survey of hybrid owners, the number one reason they drive one is to save the environment. The number two? Not surprisingly, gasoline costs. "You focus on the big picture," says Appel and keep your eye on what may lie ahead—so you can be ready for anything.

FAST FACT

THE MOST EXPENSIVE CAR IN THE WORLD? THE BUGATTI VEYRON, WHICH SELLS FOR MORE THAN A MILLION DOLLARS, GOES AS FAST AS 250 MPH, AND FEATURES A DIAMOND-INLAID SPEEDOMETER.

18. Are You Good Enough to Yourself?

You take great care of your family and friends—but most women's biggest complaint is that they don't have enough time for themselves! "Yet being good to ourselves is crucial to maintaining our emotional well-being," says Alan Siebert, PhD, author of *The Survivor Personality*. Our quiz will help you discover whether you could be nicer to yourself—and give you tips for squeezing in the TLC you deserve!

1. **If you're not in the mood to cook, you order takeout:**
   a. Always
   b. Sometimes
   c. Rarely

2. **When there's a movie you're dying to see, you catch it before it leaves the local theater:**
   a. Most of the time
   b. Sometimes
   c. Practically never—you see the DVD

3. **When someone compliments you:**
   a. You love it!
   b. It makes you bashful and you quietly say, "Thank you"
   c. You feel embarrassed and change the subject

4. **When you sit for a minute, you get the feeling that you should be doing something around the house:**
   a. Rarely
   b. Sometimes
   c. Always

5. **You treat yourself to dessert—without worrying about calories:**
   a. Always
   b. Sometimes
   c. Rarely

6. **If an inexpensive treat strikes your fancy, you buy it for yourself:**
   a. Usually
   b. Sometimes
   c. Rarely

7. **When you have a cold, you get right into bed to rest:**
   a. Always—and for as long as you need
   b. When you have a spare moment
   c. Never! There's no time for that, you have too much to do!

8. **You make it a point to get together with your girlfriends:**
   a. Regularly
   b. When you can squeeze it in
   c. Not that often

9. **You read books or magazines for pleasure:**
   a. All the time
   b. Sometimes
   c. Only once in a while

YOUR SCORE

NOTE: If your answers fall equally between the two categories, read both descriptions, since you share characteristics of both types.

MOSTLY A'S:
You're truly your own best friend!

You intuitively understand that to be good to others, you need to be good to yourself, too, otherwise you could end up burning out fast. That's why you make sure to schedule time to pamper yourself or enjoy some quiet time. "You've learned to put your own peace of mind first, overlook the small stuff, and still make plenty of time for others," says Siebert. While you're great at big indulgences, when time is tight, you're not always sure how to squeeze in a quick treat. Just:

- Buy yourself some flowers—any variety will do. Studies show just looking at fresh flower arrangements will raise your feel-good endorphins and put you in a great mood.
- Wear something sunny. "Yellow makes you feel good about yourself and the world," says color expert Leatrice Eiseman, author of *Color Your Mood*.

MOSTLY B'S:
You're a natural juggler!

On most days, you do a good job balancing your responsibilities with your own needs. But when your schedule is extra jam-packed, you tend to put yourself second, third, or fourth on the list—especially if something you need seems a little impractical. So, what would make you feel extra-pampered is for everyone to recognize how much you do for them, says Siebert. To get the credit that will make you feel good:

- Speak up. Experts say simply pointing out your own job well done to others will help you feel your effort was worth it.
- Take a hiatus. "See how quickly others appreciate your selfless habits once you take a break from your boundless good deeds," advises Siebert.

MOSTLY C'S:
You could use some TLC!

You give 110 percent of yourself to everything. And while you do get an occasional moment to yourself, even then you allow everything to distract you from taking care of your own needs. "This can leave you feeling depleted physically and emotionally," says Siebert. The solution? Remind yourself that taking time for yourself recharges you so you can do more for your loved ones later. Then, try:

- Setting aside "me" time each day. "Journal-keeping or reading are effective ways to recharge your spirit," says Siebert.
- Treating yourself to something special. A reward reminds you of how important your efforts are.

FAST FACT

WE'RE A MODEST NATION: RESEARCH SHOWS THE MAJORITY OF AMERICANS WOULD RATHER GIVE COMPLIMENTS THAN RECEIVE THEM!

19. What's Your Emotional Climate?

Are you eternally sunny? Or are you given to thundering gray moods? Everyone around you is affected by your emotional climate, so isn't it time you discovered your personal weather report?

1. **Your friend forgets your birthday. You:**
   a. Ignore it
   b. "Forget" hers when it rolls around
   c. Reconsider your friendship

2. **An unpopular coworker insults you. You:**
   a. Shrug it off
   b. Stew until you can let it go
   c. Snap back

3. **A teller applying her makeup keeps you and everyone else in the bank line waiting. You:**
   a. Go to the automatic cash machine
   b. Mention it to the bank manager on your way out
   c. Speak up and tell her to do her job!

4. **Just as you're running to catch the bus, it pulls away. The next thing you do is:**
   a. Sit down and catch your breath
   b. Hail a cab
   c. Voice your displeasure!

5. **A friend flirts with your man. You consider this:**
   a. A compliment
   b. Possible trouble ahead
   c. The end of your friendship

6. **Your face is most likely to turn red from:**
   a. The sun
   b. Embarrassment
   c. Anger

7. **The clothes you wear most often are:**
   a. Soft pastels
   b. Dark neutrals
   c. Flashy brights

YOUR SCORE

NOTE: If your answers fall equally between the two categories, read both descriptions, since you share characteristics of both types.

MOSTLY A'S:
You stay calm and cool

Even when the pressure rises above the boiling point and people around you are running in circles. This can be a real plus when you're trying to accomplish a diplomatic task. However, your casual attitude is sometimes misconstrued. Friends and lovers could think you're uncaring or blasé. You need to be more forthcoming when it comes to putting voice to your emotions.

MOSTLY B'S:
You have patience and good grace.

During the occasional lovers' spat, you're always able to think things through and find the true meaning behind your feelings and actions and those of others. Although your emotional climate is on the tame side, your sensual self is always ready and eager to be sparked. What an ideal combination for living life to the fullest!

MOSTLY C'S:
Ouch! Your hot temper flares up often enough to start a fire!

Whether it's with family, friends, lovers, even strangers, you let them know it! Lengthen that fuse by developing some self-awareness and patience. Next time you feel your temper flaring, count to ten, take a deep breath, and think about why you're so angry. With understanding comes calm.

20. Which Colors Accentuate Your Social Self?

Whether they're your favorites or not, you can boost your mood, social skills—even your health—by surrounding yourself with hues that match your personality, says Rosemary Sadez Friedmann, author of *The Mystery of Color*. Take this quiz to discover yours!

1. **Of these, the trait that's most important to you is:**
   a. Honesty
   b. Patience
   c. Compassion
   d. Creativity

2. **If you were invited to try something you'd never done before, like ride a snowmobile or a motorcycle, you'd:**
   a. Think about it for a second, then go for it
   b. Weigh the pros and cons forever
   c. Ask your closest friend's opinion first
   d. Grab the opportunity without hesitation

3. **You spend the most time in the:**
   a. Kitchen
   b. Bedroom
   c. Family room
   d. Home office

4. **If you were making a craft or recipe that wasn't coming out right, you'd probably:**
   a. Keep at it, referring to the directions for help
   b. Give it up; it's not worth stressing over
   c. Think about who you know who might be able to help
   d. Invent your own way of finishing the project

5. **On a sunny day, you'd rather:**
   a. Take a brisk walk
   b. Lounge around
   c. Get together with family or friends
   d. Dive into your favorite hobby

6. **Your prefer the scent of:**
   a. Citrus
   b. Light floral
   c. Essential oils such as patchouli or musk
   d. Vanilla or spice

7. **When you read something interesting or useful, you:**
   a. File it in your mind for future use
   b. Intend to remember it, but usually forget some of the details
   c. Tell everyone you know about it
   d. Google for more information on the subject

YOUR SCORE

NOTE: If your answers fall equally between the two categories, read both descriptions, since you share characteristics of both types.

MOSTLY A'S:
Surround yourself with BRIGHT YELLOWS!

Full of life, you'll feel your best by keeping lots of golden hues on hand—colors that match your optimistic personality! "Yellow enhances your joyful nature because it signals that emotional openness that makes you feel in your element," Friedmann says.

MOSTLY B'S:
Surround yourself with SOFT PASTELS!

High-energy shades such as yellow or green will make you feel anxious. Instead, wearing pastel clothes or painting a favorite room a delicate hue will eliminate stress. With your calm demeanor you'll thrive with plenty of soft tones around you.

MOSTLY C'S:
Surround yourself with EARTH TONES!

"Symbols of warmth, earthy golds and browns mesh well with your grounded personality," says Friedmann. You enjoy life's simple pleasures—family and the comfort of home—so it's no wonder you feel most at ease with colors that radiate an easygoing spirit.

MOSTLY D'S:
Surround yourself with JEWEL TONES!

Your feisty personality is the perfect match for vivid greens and royal reds! "These are the most stimulating of all colors," says Friedmann. "They're the chromatic ideal for strong-willed, ambitious types who enjoy basking in the limelight!"

21. Are You Fearful of Change?

This is the age of self-improvement. Millions of us try to better ourselves. We diet, exercise, meditate, travel to exotic locales, take new jobs, switch partners, and move from state to state. Deep down, we know life without alteration is static, boring, and downright dull. But try as we might, most of us never really change.

According to a recent national poll, only about one in five Americans keeps their New Year's resolutions. And many don't even consider new possibilities. We're stuck in the sand, unable to make any moves.

Experts point to fear as the biggest obstacle preventing us from turning our lives around. According to Dennis O'Grady, PhD, author of *Taking the Fear Out of Changing*, there are five basic fears that paralyze us: fear of the unknown, commitment, failure, disapproval and—surprisingly—success! Admittedly, daring to be different can be downright frightening, but as author of the contemporary classic *Fear of Flying*, Erica Jong, warns: "If you don't risk anything, you risk even more."

This quiz is a good beginning, a safe way to find out where you stand in the cycle of positive change. Answer the questions honestly and discover whether you're stuck in a rut, on a roll, or somewhere in-between. If you're having a tough time making a move, we'll offer tips on how to jumpstart your stalled life!

1. **You're most likely to be dreaming about:**
   a. Flying over a familiar town, mistress of all you survey
   b. Walking through a room you never knew existed—in your own house
   c. Finding yourself unprepared for an important event, feeling nervous and self-conscious

2. **You're spending the weekend in a secluded cabin nestled beside a lake in a forest. You definitely won't leave behind:**
   a. A journal and lots of film
   b. Hiking boots and a swimsuit
   c. Your cell phone and laptop

3. **When the alarm rings, you:**
   a. Press the snooze button and pull the covers over your head
   b. Rise immediately, wondering what the day will bring
   c. Lie awake making a mental list of activities for the day

4. **For your birthday, you'd rather have:**
   a. Amnesia
   b. Dinner in your favorite restaurant with a loved one
   c. A surprise party thrown in your honor

5. **Whenever you think about your life, you:**
   a. Feel unbelievably blessed
   b. Wonder what it would be like to be famous and rich
   c. Feel regret over lost opportunities

6. **Fantasies often take flight before a plane's liftoff. While boarding, you usually think about:**
   a. Gliding gently into a sunny paradise
   b. A terrorist takeover or a crash landing
   c. Sitting next to an interesting stranger

7. **You weigh yourself (be honest!):**
   a. About once a week
   b. At the doctor's office
   c. Once a day

8. **The last time you made a change in your hairstyle was when:**
   a. The cordless phone was invented
   b. *ER* was canceled
   c. Madonna was a brunette

9. **In most of the pictures in your family album, you are:**
   a. Center stage and hamming it up
   b. Caught in a candid and casual pose
   c. Not there. You always insist on being the photographer.

10. **When you see makeovers in magazines you:**
    a. Contemplate getting one, but haven't mustered enough courage
    b. Think they always make the woman look worse
    c. Use some of the tips offered to update your own look

11. **Your nail polish:**
    a. Looks natural— you prefer to be understated
    b. Matches your lipstick
    c. Is the latest shade, whether it's deep blue or fire-engine red

12. **What is the first question you ask yourself when choosing an outfit:**
    a. "Is it practical and comfortable?"
    b. "Will it win compliments?"
    c. "Does it cover my figure flaws?"

13. **When you are working, you watch the clock:**
    a. Constantly
    b. At slack times
    c. Never

14. **At the end of a working day, you feel:**
    a. Sometimes tired, but usually pretty satisfied
    b. Glad that you can now start really living
    c. Exhausted and desperate to relax

15. **When you make new acquaintances and they ask what you do for a living, you:**
    a. Describe your work in detail
    b. Lie and pretend you have a different gig
    c. Gloss over the subject

16. **Your job:**
    a. Underutilizes your ability
    b. Makes you accomplish things you never thought you would ever do
    c. Strains your ability

17. **How much of your work time is spent making personal telephone calls or with other matters not connected with the job?**
    a. Very little
    b. Quite a lot
    c. Some, especially at crisis times in your personal life

18. **If you suddenly inherited a large sum of money, you would:**
    a. Quit and see the world
    b. Take up some kind of work that you've always wanted to do
    c. Continue with the same work. You can't imagine doing anything else.

19. **How often have you felt or said, "Men are all the same?"**
    a. Often   b. Rarely   c. Sometimes

20. **How often do you apologize to a friend or colleague when you know you're not wrong?**
    a. Often
    b. Occasionally
    c. Rarely or never

21. **When your man isn't responding to you romantically, you:**
    a. Explore different avenues of intimacy—perhaps a walk or a massage
    b. Automatically feel rejected and depressed
    c. Assume he has other things on his mind

22. **Your thoughts about falling in love at first sight:**
    a. Well, anything is possible.
    b. A lot of Hollywood-inspired hooey.
    c. Absolute fact. It's happened to you at least once!

23. **Have you ever come to like someone you initially disliked?**
    a. Sometimes
    b. Often. You're open.
    c. Never! First impressions are indelible.

24. **When someone you know well behaves in a surprising way, you:**
    a. Take a vivid interest in this new development
    b. Feel puzzled and at a loss—but you're willing to try and understand what is going on
    c. Think he or she must have gone crazy and stay clear

YOUR SCORE

Give yourself the following number of points for each answer:

1. a-3, b-5, c-0
2. a-3, b-5, c-0
3. a-3, b-5, c-0
4. a-0, b-3, c-5
5. a-5, b-3, c-0
6. a-3, b-0, c-5
7. a-3, b-5, c-0
8. a-0, b-3, c-5
9. a-3, b-5, c-0
10. a-3, b-5, c-0
11. a-0, b-3, c-5
12. a-0, b-5, c-3
13. a-0, b-3, c-5
14. a-5, b-0, c-3
15. a-5, b-0, c-3
16. a-3, b-5, c-0
17. a-5, b-0, c-3
18. a-5, b-3, c-0
19. a-0, b-5, c-3
20. a-0, b-3, c-5
21. a-5, b-0, c-3
22. a-5, b-0, c-3
23. a-3, b-5, c-0
24. a-5, b-3, c-0

100 TO 120 POINTS:
You're on a roll.

You deeply understand what the great Eleanor Roosevelt meant when she said, "You must do the very thing you think you cannot do." You are courageous because you truly believe life always

turns out for the best. You find the silver lining in the most trying circumstances. Not surprisingly, countless psychological studies prove that optimism like yours is the greatest motivator for change. A hopeful attitude buffers people against apathy and stagnation.

University of Kansas psychologist C. R. Snyder, who developed a scale for optimism and hope, says, "Believing you have both the will and the way to accomplish your goals—whatever they may be—leads to positive change." So, stay open and upbeat and your inner glow will continue to lead the way.

75 TO 99 POINTS:
You're revving your wheels.

You're poised for change, with your pedal to the metal, but anxiety and worry keep you from shifting into high gear and going the distance. You're correct in thinking that drastically altering your lifestyle isn't something to be taken lightly. But a radical change in thinking may be just what you need to see results. Keep fear under control by visualizing positive outcomes. See yourself achieving your goals. You certainly possess all you need to succeed. Fear is the only thing holding you back. Let go of it—and you'll break the barrier to change.

LESS THAN 75 POINTS:
You're stuck in a rut.

Uncertainty makes you uneasy. You're the kind of person who feels most comfortable when you know exactly what to expect. But in reality, you've created a cocoon that limits you from experienc-

ing all that life has to offer. And somewhere inside, there's probably a little voice urging you to explore your potential. This means change! If you're too fearful to make major strides, consider taking small steps first. Try these: Take a different route home from work, awaken early enough to see the sunrise, try an exotic dish, register for an adult education course, explore a museum, learn a new software program, or introduce yourself to a stranger. Believing you can control your future is an illusion anyway. So, try to let go of it by dipping your toe into the sea of change. One day, you'll be ready to take the plunge and ride the wave.

FAST FACT

Metathesiophobia is the word meaning "fear of change"!

22. Do You Court Danger?

Do you get a kick out of tempting fate? Take this revealing quiz and find out if your lust for thrills could get you into hot water.

Part One

1. **When you see an adorable pooch tethered to his leash, you:**
   a. Steer clear. Even the cutest canines can put the bite on you.
   b. Rush over and pat him
   c. Approach slowly, and let him come to you

2. **How do you feel about steamy sex in books, movies, magazines, and on the Net?**
   a. Interested in a detached way
   b. Turned off
   c. Fascinated—you can't wait to get your mate alone!

3. **Lucky you! You just won a contest for a make-over—complete with a new hairdo that includes hair extensions and highlighting. You:**
   a. Go for it
   b. Forget it
   c. Consider it

4. **Bravely, you walk to the edge of an extremely high diving board—but once there, realize it's more of a jump than you thought. And there's a line waiting behind you. You:**
   a. Close your eyes, hold your nose, and jump
   b. Say a short, silent prayer and then do your most difficult dive
   c. Turn around and back out (and down!) gracefully

5. **Your hostess has left a bottle of extremely expensive French perfume on her bathroom counter. You:**
   a. Admire the bottle
   b. Lift out the stopper and inhale deeply
   c. Hmmm ... dab some on your wrist, neck, and earlobes

6. **"Bad news!" That's the message your best friend's been sending about the man you've been dating. You:**
   a. Ignore her; she's just jealous.
   b. Assume she's right and tell him to take a hike
   c. Heed her warning and proceed with caution

7. **To attract attention you wear:**
   a. Big, jingly jewelry
   b. Loud, electric colors
   c. Sensual, sinewy fabrics

8. **Encountering an empty stretch of highway, your date floors the pedal. You sense:**
   a. Alarm at first—but then you realize he's in complete command and you relax.
   b. Fear! You scream, "Slow down!"
   c. Apprehension, which quickly turns to excitement

Part Two

Which of these chances would you take?

1. **Leaving a lover before you find another.**
   Yes_____ No_____

2. Making love outdoors.

   Yes_____   No_____

3. Asking a cute but married coworker out for a drink.

   Yes_____   No_____

4. Playing blackjack at a casino and betting a wad.

   Yes_____   No_____

5. Traveling alone in a foreign country where you don't speak the language.

   Yes_____   No_____

YOUR SCORE

For Part One, give yourself the following number of points for each answer:

1. a-3, b-7, c-5	5. a-3, b-5, c-7
2. a-5, b-3, c-7	6. a-7, b-3, c-5
3. a-7, b-3, c-5	7. a-5, b-7, c-3
4. a-5, b-7, c-3	8. a-5, b-3, c-7

- For Part Two, give yourself 3 points for each "yes."

- Add the scores from Parts One and Two.

39 POINTS OR LESS: You're a Doubter.

Safety first—that's how you maneuver through life's more difficult hurdles. You always look both ways before crossing the street, exercise in moderation, and approach lovers with your heart on hold. Although this tactic works well most of the time, it does mean you occasionally miss out on some exciting opportunities. While it's true that haste can make waste, you have to know when it's the best time to seize the moment. Try some risk-taking. It's bound to add highlights to an otherwise humdrum day!

40 TO 55 POINTS: You're a danger dabbler.

Every now and then, you like to take a chance—but only when there's no risk to your personal safety. Emotionally, you're willing to put your heart on the line even if this sometimes means it gets a bit bruised. But not to worry: because of your zest for life, you heal easily. Your real thrill comes from sports—nothing pleases you more than a good competitive game of tennis, golf, or bowling. You enjoy traveling—in luxury—and often take off on the spur of the moment. Since you believe life is a gamble, you like to take chances. Because of your carefully monitored courage, we bet you always come up a winner!

56 POINTS OR MORE: You're a daredevil.

Nothing puts the fire under you faster than the thrill of danger. Rack it up to your insatiable appetite for adventure. Why, you could make Evel Knievel look cautious! Nothing makes you crazier than boredom, so you're willing to risk your heart and your career rather than settle down to a mundane existence. Living in the fast lane is fine—but may we suggest you exercise the teeniest bit of caution: keep your eyes wide open and occasionally apply those brakes. What you see as a little bump up ahead in the road may actually be Mount Everest!

23. Are You Too Demanding?

Do you expect all your desires to be met—right now? Take this quiz and see if you want too much!

Part One

1. **Your love nest has grown cold. You:**
   a. Tell your hubby to generate some heat
   b. Assume his lack of desire is temporary and wait patiently
   c. Melt his reserve with seductive pleasures

2. **How long will you wait at a restaurant before being served?**
   a. About fifteen minutes.
   b. It depends on the order.
   c. Within the hour.

3. **When your sitter cancels because her heartthrob finally asked her out, you say:**
   a. "I was sixteen once—have a terrific time!"
   b. "So long, kiddo, we're hiring another sitter."
   c. "Give several days notice next time, so we can get a replacement."

4. **After dieting for three and a half weeks, you've lost five pounds. What do you conclude?**
   a. Slow and steady is the way to stay slim.
   b. You need to cut back on more calories.
   c. This diet is a disaster!

5. **If you have to put your car in the shop for a week's worth of repairs, you:**
   a. Expect friends to chauffeur you around
   b. Rent a car
   c. Ask if you can share rides into town or work

6. **You've had several dates with a guy who makes you float on Cloud Nine. You:**
   a. Drop a few hints about your future…together
   b. Just enjoy dating for now and let things take their natural course
   c. Pressure him for a commitment

7. **Your daughter feels clumsy and wants to quit ballet school. You:**
   a. Cancel the class but tell her she's being too temperamental
   b. Call her a prima donna and insist she stay
   c. Acknowledge her feelings and support her

8. **He detests liver, but you love it. You:**
   a. Serve it weekly
   b. Order it whenever you eat out
   c. Cook it when you get a craving, but serve him something else

Part Two

1. **Okay, so I'm stubborn!**
   Agree_____ Disagree_____

2. **I expect my children to always be well behaved.**
   Agree_____ Disagree_____

3. **There's no excuse for tardiness.**
   Agree_____ Disagree_____

4. **If my mate even looks at another woman, I'm furious!** Agree_____ Disagree_____

5. **Friends should be on call 24/7.**
Agree_____ Disagree_____

YOUR SCORE

- For Part One, give yourself the following number of points for each answer.

  1. a-7, b-3, c-5
  2. a-7, b-5, c-3
  3. a-3, b-7, c-5
  4. a-3, b-5, c-7
  5. a-7, b-3, c-5
  6. a-5, b-3, c-7
  7. a-5, b-7, c-3
  8. a-7, b-5, c-3

- For Part Two, give yourself 3 points for each statement with which you agree.

- Add the scores from Parts One and Two.

39 POINTS OR LESS:
You have the ability to shrug your shoulders and laugh it off...

Whether a friend misses an appointment with you, a coworker slips up on a job you share, or your kid is going wild. Although you live a relatively stress-free life, your laissez-faire attitude has its drawbacks. Since you expect very little from others, you also expect very little from yourself.

We're not suggesting you become a tyrant for perfection overnight, but your standards do need to be raised. Begin by exploring some possibilities for self-improvement. Once you meet your own potential, you're at liberty to seek the same from others.

40 TO 55 POINTS:
Generally easygoing...

You take most things in stride. When it comes to your family, friends, and lovers, you're a pussycat who prefers to forgive and forget, rather than make a big deal out of nothing. However, you have very little tolerance for poor service. If a waitress is slow, your bank makes an error, or your new washing machine breaks down, you practically blow a gasket! When you pay, you expect perfection. Basically, we agree with your philosophy, but there's no use yelling. You'll get better results if you put a damper on your fiery temper.

56 POINTS OR MORE:
You want everything in your life to run like clockwork...

And when it doesn't, you throw a fit. You also expect everyone around you to be at your beck and call. But more often than not, your demands are unrealistic. It's fine to strive for perfection, but the truth is, things rarely turn out the way you want them to. Life has its own unpredictable course. Don't demand the impossible—that way you won't be disappointed!

24. Discover Your Special Gift of Kindness

You're great at making everyone's wishes come true—especially around holidays—but "being nice to yourself can help you battle holiday stress," says Jacob Teitelbaum, MD, author of *Three Steps to Happiness*.

1. **You love to crawl into bed wearing:**
   a. A soft nightgown
   b. An oversized T-shirt
   c. A beautiful teddy or camisole
   d. Your mate's PJs

2. **When you're a passenger on a long car trip, you prefer to:**
   a. Snooze
   b. Chat
   c. Check out the scenery
   d. Be the navigator

3. **The beauty item you're never without is:**
   a. Moisturizer
   b. Mascara
   c. Nail polish
   d. Lipstick

4. **Of these, your favorite Christmas carol is:**
   a. "Silent Night"
   b. "Rockin' Around the Christmas Tree"
   c. "Little Drummer Boy"
   d. "Santa Claus Is Coming to Town"

5. **Your dream house is:**
   a. Victorian
   b. Modern
   c. Tudor
   d. Ranch

6. **What's most prominently posted on your refrigerator door?**
   a. School schedules and community notices
   b. Pictures of friends and family
   c. Inspirational quotes
   d. Grocery lists

YOUR SCORE:

NOTE: If your answers fall equally between the two categories, read both descriptions, since you share characteristics of both types.

MOSTLY A'S:
You should give yourself EXTRA TIME IN BED.

Sleeping in is the perfect gift for your type-A personality because you see time for yourself as the ultimate luxury. Plus, "research shows that when you get less than eight hours sleep, everything form your patience to your complexion suffers," says Teitelbaum.

MOSTLY B'S:
You should give yourself A NIGHT OUT WITH THE GALS.

You get emotional and mental sustenance from being with friends—and when your days feel nonstop, that's when you need these connections most. "Studies prove social ties keep you healthier," says Teitelbaum.

MOSTLY C'S:

You should give yourself A SPECIAL PRESENT.

"The easiest way to feel deprived and resentful at this time of year is to neglect yourself," says Teitelbaum. That's why generous types like you should be kind to yourself. Go ahead and get that little item you've had your eye on. Even wrap it, and put it under the tree to increase the magic of Christmas Day!

MOSTLY D'S:

You should give yourself ANYTHING THAT MAKES ENTERTAINING EASIER.

There's no better reward for a take-charge perfectionist like you than permission to use a shortcut. So go ahead, buy prepared foods, premade decorations, and anything that helps with our holiday entertaining. "Cutting yourself some slack will let you get the joy from the holidays that you deserve," says Teitelbaum.

25. What's Your Unique Allure?

1. **You're on a job interview and you want to win over your prospective employer. You:**
    a. Share a personal anecdote that shows you in a positive light
    b. Compliment her on the family photo on her desk or on the way she's decorated her office
    c. Maintain comfortable eye contact while you're answering all her questions

2. **You walk into a party where the only person you recognize is the hostess. To get to know the other guests, you:**
    a. Go from group to group and engage people in conversation
    b. Introduce yourself to one or two guests, encouraging them to open up
    c. Volunteer to help the hostess serve cocktails and introduce yourself to guests along the way

3. **You're trying to get a loan approval for your Bake-a-Brownie business. You help convince the loan officer by:**
    a. Exuding confidence with your best smile
    b. Presenting her with a complimentary box of your yummy brownies
    c. Showing your anticipated profit margin and a statement of your long-range business strategies

4. **You're in a very long line at the supermarket, and the other customers are getting cranky. To make the situation more tolerable, you:**
    a. Turn to the next person in line and make a few humorous comments about the situation
    b. Nod your head in sympathetic agreement to some of the louder complaints

c. Go to the store manager and ask him to open another checkout lane

5. **Which career appeals to you most?**
   a. Cruise director
   b. Counselor or therapist
   c. Teacher

6. **If you were running for political office, you'd garner votes by:**
   a. Working the crowd with your warm and appealing personality
   b. Running a grassroots campaign, listening carefully to voters' concerns
   c. Focusing mainly on the most pressing issues

YOUR SCORE

NOTE: If your answers fall equally between two categories, read both descriptions, since you share characteristics of two types.

MOSTLY A'S:
You're outgoing.

Your outgoing nature is the key to your charisma. People love to be around you because of your upbeat attitude. Your optimistic and enthusiastic approach encourages others to relax and support you in your efforts. It's no wonder your social schedule is so busy—you're the life of everyone's party!

MOSTLY B'S:
You're sympathetic.

Your charismatic secret is your ability to be a great listener. Inevitably, people are drawn to this important quality. Warm and sympathetic, you're naturally open and compassionate. Your sweet, sensitive nature is what makes you irresistible!

MOSTLY C'S:
You're a straight-shooter.

You're strong and self-assured, and valued for these qualities. You're not one to beat around the bush, and people are attracted to you because of your direct approach. They trust you and appreciate the confidence you exude. Since it's obvious that you believe in yourself, others believe in you as well.

26. Which Hero Inspires You Most?

There's nothing like the sight of a man in uniform—so strong, yet so caring—to make us feel protected and reassured. As they put their lives on the line to keep our homes, our families, towns, cities, states, and this nation safe, these brave men earn our respect and admiration. And even if you feel you could never be one-tenth as brave as they are, psychologists say that those very qualities you admire are inside of you, too. "Each one of these American heroes stands for a very special kind of strength," says psychologist Neil Clark Warren, PhD, founder of eHarmony.com. The one you relate to most reveals your own inner heroism—your connection and dedication to others.

FIREFIGHTER:
You keep others cool.

There's a reason firefighters are called "America's Bravest": there's no one more willing to race into danger to rescue others. "Doing so requires not just strength, but a level-headed calm that encourages others to feel safe and follow their lead," says Warren. "It's this calm that attracts you, because that's the way you like to live your own life!" A natural diplomat, you know how to defuse any situation quickly and decisively. Your reassuring manner makes you the one friends seek out for advice—because the confidence you provide is enough to cool even the most heated dispute.

MARINE, ARMY OFFICER, GREEN BERET:
You're a team player.

"These brave warriors—defenders of our nation all over the world—keep America strong through their steadfast loyalty, teamwork, and faithfulness. And if they're your choice, it's probably because that's how you live your life, too," explains Warren. Flexible and receptive, you enjoy the friendship and closeness that develops when you collaborate with others. And your family is your favorite team—because you know that a caring, close-knit bond is the key to weathering any storm.

EMT:
You never stop learning.

With their quick thinking and desire to heal, EMTs save thousands of lives every year—because they know just what to do when everyone else is panicking. "This cool approach is the result of intensive training," says Warren, "and chances are, you share this love of knowledge!" You have a deep need to understand things and know that learning something new every day is the key to a successful future.

POLICE OFFICER:
You solve tough problems.

Called "America's Finest," our men in blue are the everyday heroes who keep our country running smoothly. They keep us free from fear by bravely putting their lives on the line in any type of emergency. "Just like police officers—whose job requires them to solve a variety of problems quickly—you're blessed with a keen insight that helps you find the best solution to any situation," explains Warren. In fact, instead of seeing problems as stumbling blocks, you view them as challenges. Friends, family, and coworkers often turn to you because they know you're always on duty and willing to lend a hand.

NAVAL OFFICER:
You've got depth.

Those ocean-going protectors spend long periods away from home, watching land from a distance, planning secret missions, and preparing for combat. "Because of this, naval officers see life from a more philosophical perspective—in many ways, as wide and deep as the ocean," says Warren. And if you relate to them, so do you! Though you enjoy being surrounded by loved ones, you also find it helpful to spend time alone writing in your journal or meditating. Your wait-and-see approach to life is why you're almost always correct in the way you see the world.

AIR FORCE PILOT:
You're forward-thinking.

Military pilots are not only some of the most courageous heroes around, but because precision and planning leads to successful Air Force missions, these defenders of the skies are highly intelligent and extremely patient. "Just like them, you plan for the future, paying attention to detail so you'll be prepared for any event," says Warren. Friends think of you as polished and extremely organized and with that winning combination, when it comes to handling pressure—the sky's the limit.

27. Are You Resilient?

"We're all born with a capacity to bounce back from life's setbacks, but how easy it will be depends on whether you're naturally optimistic, self-confident, and flexible," says Beth Miller, author of *The Woman's Book of Resilience.* **Take this quiz and find your resiliency factor—and learn strategies to boost your recovery skills.**

1. **If you were hoping for a promotion, but a coworker got it instead, you would most likely:**
    a. Look at the bright side: at least you won't have to put in extra hours
    b. Wish her the best and vow to do whatever it takes to get the next promotion
    c. Take yourself out for lunch because you deserve a pick-me-up

2. **If your local store were out of your favorite cereal, you would:**
    a. Drive to another store
    b. Buy a different cereal
    c. Check back in a day or so

3. **When you've had an argument with someone close, you typically respond by:**
    a. Apologizing
    b. Asking her what you can do to fix things
    c. Feeling sad as you wait to see what happens

4. **You hate your new haircut! What do you do?**
    a. Shrug it off. Hair grows back.
    b. Analyze what went wrong—and ask the hairdresser to make some changes
    c. Wear a hat for a while

5. **You choose a bonbon from an assorted box of chocolates and you don't like it, so you:**
    a. Look at the size and shape and choose a completely different one
    b. Toss it but consider the error a blessing; you won't be tempted to eat more!
    c. Keep tasting whichever ones look appealing until you're satisfied

6. **You're at a meeting where a coworker takes credit for work that you did. You:**
    a. Wait until she finished speaking then thank her for referencing your work
    b. Take the colleague aside later and tell her in the future you expect her to give you the credit you deserve
    c. Be grateful that at least now you know you can't trust her!

7. **The last time you were stuck in traffic on your way to work, you thought:**
    a. "Tomorrow I'll wake up ten minutes earlier."
    b. "I knew I shouldn't have taken this route."
    c. "My supervisor is going to be annoyed."

YOUR SCORE

NOTE: If your answers fall equally between the two categories, read both descriptions, since you share characteristics of both types.

MOSTLY A'S:
You rebound at lightening speed!

When things don't go the way you like, you just change direction! Never one to mope, you face

obstacles with optimism and a focus on the future. "You rebound so fast because you believe everything ultimately works out for the best," says Miller. But you may be so quick to recover that you often don't give yourself time to reflect and learn from your mistakes. So to make the absolute best of a bad situation:

- Vent. Even if you let off steam by crying or yelling in any empty room, studies show it has a healing effect physically and emotionally.
- Ask for support from a trusted friend or family member. Talking through your disappointment with a supportive buddy can make you feel better not only about what went wrong but also about your new direction.

MOSTLY B'S: You can be competitive.

You accept life's letdowns with a healthy attitude because you can see the light at the end of the tunnel. But your competitive nature makes it harder for you to quickly rebound when others get ahead of you. "That's when you have to really work at it, making sure not to lick your wounds for too long," says Miller. To win back your confidence:

- Be philosophical. Keep a sticky note with the words, "The tortoise wins the race." It will help you envision a positive outcome, raising your level of optimism.
- Pursue a hobby. Doing something you're good at boosts your self-esteem and helps you move on.

MOSTLY C'S:
You take things to heart!

As a sensitive soul resistant to change, when you face setbacks, you need some time to rebound. "Instead of seeing some things as beyond your control, you take disappointments personally and need time to readjust," says Miller. The way to let things roll off your back:

- Be grateful. When things don't go your way, make a list of what you have to be thankful for—family, friends, work—and it will help you move through setbacks.
- Laugh at jokes or funny movies. When your sense of humor is activated, you feel invigorated to take on new challenges.

28. *The Secrets Hidden under Your Covers!*

"Everything about your sleep—from your favorite sleeping position to how you rest and what you dream about—can speak volumes about the kind of person you are," says Paul Glovinsky, PhD, author of *The Insomnia Answer.*

1. **Your most comfortable sleeping position is:**
   a. On your back
   b. On your side
   c. On your stomach

2. **On weeknights, your bedtime is typically:**
   a. Around midnight—or later
   b. Between ten and eleven
   c. Before ten

3. **In the half hour before bed, you'd be most likely to:**
   a. Watch television or read
   b. Unwind in a hot bath
   c. Lay out your clothes for the next day

4. **Your favorite thing to wear to bed is:**
   a. An oversized T-shirt
   b. A nightgown or lingerie
   c. PJs

5. **Your remember your dreams:**
   a. Sometimes
   b. Often
   c. Never

6. **In terms of temperature, you sleep best in a bedroom that's:**
   a. Cool
   b. Warm and toasty
   c. Neither too hot nor too cold

7. **You're usually awakened in the morning by:**
   a. Your own natural body clock
   b. Sunlight coming through the windows
   c. An alarm clock

YOUR SCORE

NOTE: If your answers fall equally between the two categories, read both descriptions, since you share characteristics of both types.

MOSTLY A'S:
You have boundless energy!

Any time of the day or night, your mind is jam packed with thoughts, and you're usually busy trying to cross one last thing off your to-do list. No wonder you often have trouble falling asleep! A natural juggler who thrives on having lots to do, you can get by with much less sleep than most of the people around you!

MOSTLY B'S:
You're a sentimental softie!

You like to be nurtured as much as you thrive on caring for those around you. "You're the ultimate sentimental soul who values feelings—especially love—above all else and has no trouble putting herself in someone else's shoes," says Glovinsky. You trust your heart first and foremost, and you never lose sleep over your decisions.

MOSTLY C'S:
You're a no-nonsense doer!

Your motto: There's a place for everything and everything in its place. And that includes sleep. So it's no surprise that even on the most chaotic day, you still get a solid eight hours of shut-eye—without tossing or turning! "Whereas others may let emotions rule, you handle nearly every situation with a level head," says Glovinsky.

29. Which Fairy-Tale Princess Are You?

Your choice Reveals Your Hopes and Dreams!

What girl didn't grow up wishing she was a princess? But did you know that the one you relate to most today reveals your hopes and dreams? Take this quiz and discover your inner princess!

1. **Of these authors, you'd be more likely to read:**
   a. Stephen King
   b. Danielle Steel
   c. David Sedaris

2. **You'd buy an alarm clock that woke you up with:**
   a. Ringing or buzzing
   b. Nature sounds such as ocean waves
   c. The radio

3. **Your dream car is a:**
   a. Fully loaded SUV
   b. Sporty convertible such as a Porsche
   c. Luxury car such as a Jaguar

4. **You record most of your phone numbers:**
   a. On your cell phone
   b. In your phone book
   c. On scraps of paper or in your head

5. **You've got a spare hour in the evening, so you use it to:**
   a. Start a project you've been dying to do
   b. Cozy up in front of the TV or with your honey
   c. Zone out in a warm bath

6. **If you had an extra hundred dollars to spend, you'd plan a:**
   a. Shopping trip
   b. Special night with your guy
   c. Spa day

7. **You'd love to receive a bouquet of:**
   a. Wildflowers
   b. Long-stemmed roses
   c. Bright tulips

8. **When it's chilly in your house, you usually warm up with a:**
   a. Sweater or sweatshirt
   b. Wrap or throw
   c. Cozy robe

YOUR SCORE

NOTE: If your answers fall equally between the two categories, read both descriptions, since you share characteristics of both types.

MOSTLY A'S:
You're SNOW WHITE

Few princesses loved a challenge more than Snow White—after all, she took on those Seven Dwarfs!

"Women who identify with Snow White are always ready to put their wits to the test with a new challenge," says Cary J. Broussard, author of *From Cinderella to CEO.*

MOSTLY B'S:
You're CINDERELLA!

"On the outside you're all about taking care of others, but on the inside, you live for romance, just like Cinderella!" says Broussard. And you'll get just what you want if you rally loved ones to pitch in—giving you time for a romantic evening for two!

MOSTLY C'S:
You're SLEEPING BEAUTY!

"Just like Sleeping Beauty, you have trouble saying no to anything that sounds interesting," says Broussard. But women like you who do too much, deep down crave a simpler, more relaxing life.

Ever wonder how some people stay calm during the craziest times? "It could be they were born that way. Studies show some of us are genetically programmed to have mellow temperaments," says Jay Winner, MD, author of *Stress Management Made Simple: Effective Ways to Beat Stress for Better Health.* **Take this quiz and find out if you've got the "mellow gene"—and learn how to live a calmer life!**

1. **When it comes to sleep, you typically:**
    a. Get at least seven to eight hours a night
    b. Get barely five to six hours a night

2. **On highways, you usually drive:**
    a. At or below the speed limit
    b. At least five to seven miles over the speed limit

3. **When you sit down to dinner, you're usually:**
    a. One of the last to leave the table
    b. One of the first to finish eating

4. **Do you suffer from headaches or upset stomach?**
    a. Rarely   b. Sometimes

5. **Your work space at home and the office are:**
    a. Cluttered   b. Organized

6. **When you feel like a snack, you most often crave something:**
    a. Hearty   b. Sweet

7. **When you have a free hour, you're likely to:**
    a. Do something fun, or even lazy
    b. Tackle a task around the house

8. **If there were a disagreement among loved ones, you'd most likely:**
   a. Wait a while, believing it will work itself out
   b. Take the lead in getting it sorted out

9. **You're someone friends and family come to you more often when they:**
   a. Want advice
   b. Need something done

YOUR SCORE

Give yourself 5 points for each "a" answer and 2 points for each "b."

39 TO 45 POINTS:
You were born mellow!

Research shows folks like you produce higher levels of serotonin, a brain chemical that boosts feelings of well-being and optimism. "Having a sunny outlook helps you stay focused on the big picture, react calmly during crises, and take time to savor life's special moments," says Dr. Winner. It's no wonder that you get less stress-related illnesses and sleep better than most people. The only drawback: Sometimes you're so mellow that you take the backseat, even when it would be wise to grab the wheel and steer. To give yourself a boost:

- Go for a walk. Studies show walking thirty minutes a day gives you 30 percent more energy than if you sit still.

30 TO 38 POINTS:
You usually go with the flow!

When trouble hits, you've got what it takes to stay calm and collected. But it's probably not a mellow gene that keeps you so cool. "Your approach is a learned technique," says Dr. Winner. "During a crisis, you look for the cause, and solve it one step at a time." This approach is effective when others are reacting emotionally. But when it comes to day-to-day pressures, like a tight deadline or being stuck in traffic, that's when you tend to feel the heat. To reduce stress:

- Lower the bar. Research shows daily pressures can be eased by lowering expectations. Get takeout instead of cooking, put off the laundry, or delegate more often than trying to do it all yourself.

29 POINTS OR LESS: You're wired for action!

Biologically high strung and always on your toes, you've got enough energy to light a small city. Bosses, colleagues, and friends admire your spunk and willingness to take on challenges. But your stress level may be soaring—especially when plans change or there's a crisis. "Even though a certain amount of stress can be motivating, too much can affect your health and increase the potential for burnout," says Dr. Winner. To keep your nerves steady:

- Try B vitamins. Or eat foods that are enriched with them, such as fruits, nuts, and fish. B vitamins provide energy and keep your nerves rock steady.

31. What Kind of Thinker Are You?

Sure, we all think we balance our hearts, minds, and experiences when we make decisions, but one of them usually rules. "Knowing which one can reveal how you relate to the world," says psychologist Ian Robertson, author of *Mind Sculpture.*

1. **You typically shop for groceries:**
   a. Almost daily, getting a few items here and there
   b. Once a week
   c. In bulk, every other week or so

2. **The gift certificate you'd most love to receive is for:**
   a. A session with a fortune teller or astrologer
   b. A book or department store
   c. A spa treatment like a facial or massage

3. **When it comes to keeping secrets, you:**
   a. Usually keep quiet—unless you think you could help someone by sharing
   b. Never tell a soul
   c. Only tell your mate or one other confidant

4. **When it comes to breakfast, you usually eat:**
   a. Anything you're in the mood for in the moment
   b. A hearty meal, such as cereal, pancakes, or eggs
   c. Something quick, such as muffins or bagels

5. **The newscaster you'd most like to have lunch with is:**
   a. Diane Sawyer
   b. Katie Couric
   c. Barbara Walters

6. **If you boss said you could paint your work area any color, you would choose:**
   a. Soft shades, such as pale blue or lavender
   b. Neutral white
   c. Bold hues, such as maroon or deep green

7. **You favorite daytime TV shows are:**
   a. Talk shows
   b. Game shows
   c. Soaps

YOUR SCORE

NOTE: If your answers fall equally between the two categories, read both descriptions, since you share characteristics of both types.

MOSTLY A'S:
Your thinking is ruled by INTUITION.

You typically make decisions based on your gut feelings, and "studies show 75 percent of the time, folks who do this are right on target," says Robertson. Intuitive decision makers like you tend to look at the big picture, visualizing the long-term impact of whatever you decide.

MOSTLY B'S:
Your thinking is ruled by LOGIC.

You like to gather all available information and weigh the pros and cons before reaching a decision. "With a methodical mind like yours, you could never be comfortable making a snap choice," says Robertson. And because you process information quickly, taking the step-by-step approach doesn't slow you down.

MOSTLY C'S:
Your thinking is ruled by EXPERIENCE.

Analyzing or basing conclusions on hard data isn't your way. "Instead, you pay attention to your own life lessons, learning from your mistakes and moving on," says Robertson. You know what you like or what has worked in the past, and that's what you count on to make your choices today!

32. The Secrets Your Fingernails Reveal about You!

Ever notice how your friend's fingernails are long like an oval, whereas yours might be wide? Everyone is born with a different fingernail shape, and according to ancient palmistry, "That shape reveals your strongest personality traits," explains Pamelah Tablak, author of *Your Heart Is in Your Hand*. So, give yourself a hand—and discover what makes you special!

ALMOND:
You trust your sixth sense.

Feel as if something great is about to happen? "Almonds tend to be a bit psychic: they trust their intuition—and mystical power—to deal successfully with real-life issues!" says Tablak. And:

- Educators call you an "intuitive learner," someone who doesn't need directions to assemble your son's new bike or that new piece of furniture.
- You're inner directed, meaning you enjoy contemplating the meaning of life—a trait psychologists say is shared by famous writers and artists!

MIXED/ASSORTED:
You're adorably zany!

Do your fingernails come in several shapes? That's true for more than 30 percent of us! You've never lost your youthful joie de vivre, so it's no wonder that:

- You've never had a problem with stress because you use humor to relieve tension—which doctors say is a proven stress-fighter!
- Your entertaining stories put you on the A-list everywhere you go!
- People think you look years younger than your age! Why? Studies show whimsical personalities age more slowly!

RECTANGULAR:
You're a mover and shaker.

Never been able to pass up a dare? "That's because people with broad, rectangular fingernails—shaped like a spatula—tend to welcome competition and thrive on a challenge," says Tablak. And that's why:

- You'd rather be flitting from place to place than sitting in front of the television—which is why studies show folks like you spend six fewer hours in front of the set a week than the average American!
- Studies show confident, never-say-die types like you are born leaders!

SQUARE:
You're rock steady.

"This type of fingernail belongs to the classic even-keeler who prefers to stay within bounds rather than risk what they have," says Tablak. And your balanced perspective not only keeps you grounded, but it also makes you:

- A conscientious clock-watcher who's always on time!
- A whiz at decision making, since cautious folks like you rely on logic and facts to solve problems.

33. Which Shape Don't You Like?

Psychologists have known for a long time that our favorite shape reveals hidden insights about our deepest feelings—but now they say the shape you dislike is important, too! Why? "Since shapes are such basic elements of our everyday environment, they're deeply connected to our psyche: the one you avoid represents the part of your personality you don't readily show the world and may have difficulty expressing," explains shape and personality theorist Susan Dellinger, PhD, author of *Psycho-Geometrics*. So choose the design you like the least—and discover what shape you're really in!

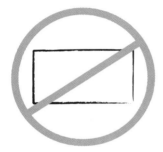

IF YOU DON'T LIKE RECTANGLES:
You're a decisive action-taker.

Research reveals that most people are drawn to rectangles when they're feeling indecisive, powerless, or in need of a change. "But studies also show just the opposite: that if you reject rectangles, you're riding a wave of take-charge power and quick-thinking confidence that puts you ahead of the game!" Dellinger says. A decisive thinker, you can survey a situation in the time it takes others to just see the problem! Always striving to do your best, you set a great example, encouraging everyone from your kids to your coworkers to give it their all.

IF YOU DON'T LIKE CIRCLES:
You're a committed friend.

Psychology studies show that for most people, the circle represents the social world and interaction with those around us (that's where we get the phrases "circle of friends" and "family circle")! "If it's your least favorite," says Dellinger, "it doesn't mean you're unsociable, just that you prefer your social whirl on a smaller scale." Loyal and committed, you choose your close friends carefully and keep them for life, cherishing them as through they were family—and your love and caring make those close to you feel honored to be in your company!

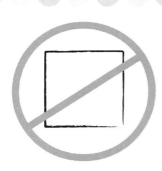

IF YOU DON'T LIKE SQUARES:
You're a free spirit.

In psychological terms, a square is called a "box," and those who are drawn to it tend to be detail-oriented list-makers who are happiest following preset paths. But if it's your least favorite, you think "outside the box!" Creative and enthusiastic, you love to let your imagination wander—and you're constantly coming up with new ways to make life fun," says Dellinger. Paint a mural in the kitchen? Plant exotic flowers in the yard? Sport a funky bikini at the local pool? Sure! With your have-a-blast attitude, you'll try all three—because there's nothing square about you!

IF YOU DON'T LIKE SQUIGGLES:
You're a happy harmonizer.

Surveys show that squiggles, which are the only individually determined shape, represent fierce indepen-

dence and the desire to choose one's own path despite the wishes of others—and that's just not your style! "You're a real relationship person who wants everyone around you to be happy," says Dellinger. A great conversationalist, you can entertain a group of strangers or lend an ear to a close friend with equal skill! Creating harmony and camaraderie wherever you go, you never forget a birthday or a friend's favorite dessert—and that's why loved ones know you're a straight arrow who shoots right for the heart!

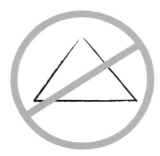

IF YOU DON'T LIKE TRIANGLES:
You're an easygoing optimist.

For hundreds of years, the triangle has symbolized powerful ambition and a yearning to reach the top at whatever cost. "But those who reject it possess a more carefree approach to life," says Dellinger. Grateful for all you have, you count your blessings every day. Your content, optimistic attitude keeps you even and calm, no matter how rocky the storm! Psychologists say this kind of emotional intelligence is an even greater predictor of success than ambition—which makes you a real winner!